Bentonville Before Wal-Mart

Bentonville Before

Wal-Mart

Growing Up in Rural Arkansas in the 1950's

Michael McFarland Knott

Illustrated by William David Martin

Dedicated To and In Memory of My Mother
Theron Mae McFarland Knott
A Woman of Few Words Who Taught Me a Lot

Contents

Illustrations

Introduction

They Only Laughed Once at Sam Walton

Early one afternoon in 1961, I was in my eleventh grade class when we heard downtown Bentonville was on fire. Several of us took advantage of the ensuing chaos, left class and ran the three blocks to downtown. We passed Percy Gailey's Phillips 66 Station, Tinnin's Drugstore, Southwest Gas and stopped in front of Snookie's Pool Hall. Several of the old-timers had left their checker game at Snookie's and were standing on the north side of Second Street watching the fire. It had completely engulfed Bank's Food Market and the surrounding businesses, with flames towering over a hundred feet in the air. Half of a city block was in flames, with only an alley keeping the conflagration from spreading to more businesses, including Sam Walton's Five and Ten.

As we watched, Sam appeared on the second story roof of Shore's Hardware above the alley. He observed the fire, disappeared and then reappeared on the south side of the hardware store. As my friend Kester later said, "Sam kept yelling at the firefighters to get up on the roof where he was." The firefighters followed his suggestion and got up on the roof where they could direct the water down on the fire.

Sam then reappeared on our side holding a garden hose. One of the old-timers standing by me snickered and then laughed.

"What is Sam thinking? He can't put out that fire with a garden hose!"

The others laughed in agreement. Sam then turned facing the other way, spraying water on the flat tar roof behind him. It became clear that Sam wasn't trying to put out the fire but rather was extinguishing burning embers falling on his roof and the surrounding businesses. He prevented the fire from spreading to the other half of the block. The garden hose was just what he needed to do that job.

At that time, the Five and Ten was Sam Walton's only store. If he had lost it to the fire that day, would it have ended his Wal-Mart plans? I doubt it, since Sam's persistence was unstoppable. That was probably the last time anyone ever laughed at Sam Walton.

***

Three thousand people lived in Bentonville, Arkansas in the 1950s, long before it became the home office of the largest corporation in the world. My youth during this time was quiet, unaware of the formidable changes to come. The time was post-World War II, the

Golden 50s and Sam and Helen Walton were just ordinary townsfolk like the rest of us. We all prayed every Sunday for our boys to come home from Korea, although I didn't know where Korea was.

Bentonville was a small town in search of its own geographic identity. Situated on the Ozark Plateau, which joined northern Arkansas and southern Missouri, most people would think it was located in "the South." Not really. It was too far north and too high to be located in the wet flatlands of the "true" South, near the Great Plains to the west but not part of it and too far west to be part of the much younger Appalachians.

Compounding its geographic ambiguity, Bentonville was isolated from any large city. The largest cities were Joplin, Missouri (60 miles), Springfield, Missouri (90 miles), Tulsa, Oklahoma (125 miles), Fort Smith, Arkansas (60 miles) and Little Rock, Arkansas (250 miles). There were no interstate highways then, so travel to any of these cities required several hours of driving. When people were asked if they had been to such-and-such city, the standard reply was, "No, I haven't lost anything there." Or more likely, "No, I ain't lost nothin' thar."

In downtown Bentonville a drop of water in the west gutter of A Street would make its way into Oklahoma, turn south in the Elk River, join the Arkansas River and flow into the Mississippi. A drop of water in the east gutter would flow north into the White River, travel up through Missouri and then back down into Arkansas to join the "Big Muddy." Then this Missouri drop would run south in the mighty

Mississippi and rejoin its kin where the Arkansas River joins the Mississippi. This confusion all began 20 feet apart in the gutters of A Street in downtown Bentonville, one block from where I grew up.

It was not just land and water that had difficulty with geographic allegiance. The politics of the area were also contentious and confusing. Old maps showed the Union in blue and the Confederacy in gray, but this area of northwest Arkansas was depicted in hatched black and white stripes. It was puzzling to a little kid. What side were we on? Had we won or lost "the Waaaar" (meaning the Civil War)?

I had always wanted to write about my childhood in Bentonville. When I was 51, I almost suffered a heart attack while mountain biking. I had already outlived my father by three years. I needed a change.

I semi-retired from ER medicine by giving up night shifts and began to write. Seventeen years and 50 stories later, I realized how different my childhood was compared with those of my children, grandchildren and most other children today.

My stories are about a curious little kid wandering around a small town, trying to escape boredom and find something to do. I explored my neighborhood, downtown Bentonville and my family's 40-acre valley, known as "Slaughter Pen Hollow." I discovered that my neighbors and townspeople had unique personalities, idiosyncrasies and interesting stories to tell. I was willing to listen. We had grown up before television told us how to act, what to wear and how to think. Their lives and mine developed in unscripted ways. Although we didn't realize it at the time, we shared a strong belief in self-expression and the freedom to be our unique selves.

When television later brought the outside world into our homes, profound social changes seized our attention. The Vietnam War was fought in our living rooms. Kennedy's assassination shocked us all. The Civil Rights and Women's Rights movements introduced new ideas that changed how we thought about equality and what we had held as truth.

Television enhanced our lives, but there were also losses, especially for young kids growing up. Our need to imagine, create and explore was killed by the click of the remote control. It happened without a fight, without us even noticing.

My stories are the record of one boy's adventures in rural, small town, 1950s America that became the birthplace of Wal-Mart. Some are mischievous, silly and comical. Others are ironic or sad. But all possess an underlying twist or a lesson learned.

My intent in writing these stories was never to cause harm to anyone and to my knowledge I have not. These stories are the truth, as I remember it. Some dialogue was created to help tell that truth.

Michael McFarland Knott
Scottsdale, Arizona
November 1, 2012

Chapter One

Family

Dad Died Before Breakfast

In 1957, I was thirteen. One morning I awoke to the sound of my parents talking in the kitchen. Usually I was the second person to wake up after Dad. An early riser, he would read the entire *St. Louis Post Dispatch*, from front page to the classifieds, between three and five in the morning. Next was the *Arkansas Gazette*, delivered around 5:30. He bought the St. Louis paper at Gus's Newsstand the previous day and carefully avoided looking at even the headlines until the wee hours of the morning. It was a treat to begin his day.

When I walked into the kitchen, Mother was making a second pot of coffee. Dad was having chest pain and had already taken two nitroglycerin tablets. Since his heart attack a year ago, he had not been well. Over the last six months he had lost 40 of his 250 pounds. With any exertion he had shortness of breath and chest pain, but it would resolve with rest and a nitroglycerin tablet.

But this episode was different. The pain continued and hadn't been relieved by the tablets. Mother seemed calm and Dad lit another cigarette. He was well into his first of three packs for the day.

Since his heart attack a year ago Dad had quit drinking. Before that he would periodically go on binges where he drank continuously, eventually ending up in his bedroom. He would emerge only to chug another glass of Old Crow Whiskey and water. I remember the bottle of Old Crow sitting on the kitchen counter. I saw the bottle as the problem and thought if it disappeared he wouldn't drink. I hid the bottle in my closet, only to see a new bottle appear the next day. I poured half of it in the sink and was about to fill it with water when Mother caught me. She said Dad would be okay in a few days.

After several days of continuous drinking and not eating, Dad began to vomit. He was ready for admission to Room 25 of Bates Memorial Hospital. No other room was acceptable—it was the last one on the hospital corridor, farthest from the nurse's station and had corner windows. He would keep drinking until it became available. After several days of drying out, he would begin his life again. Everyone in town knew Dad was "sick," and Mother kept the insurance office going until he got out of the hospital (although she didn't try to sell any new insurance policies, because only Dad could do that).

I always dreaded and feared the onset of the next binge. They usually started when my father got together with a friend and the "old times" would begin.

A year ago he had gone fishing with "Big Jim" Tinnin, the father of Jimmy Tinnin, my oldest friend. They were in Big Jim's canoe on the White River. There had been a lot of rain and the river was high. The drinking had begun and Dad was in front casting his ZebCo rod and reel toward the shore. After several casts, Dad had a pull from a bottle of Old Crow. Big Jim was casting, paddling and taking pulls from a bottle of Early Times. They rounded a tight bend in the river, causing the canoe to drift to the edge of the bank. After some poorly executed corrective attempts, the canoe went under a low hanging tree. A large cottonmouth snake fell from a branch into the canoe.

My dad was dreadfully afraid of any snake, but especially the poisonous cottonmouth. He leapt from the canoe and frantically battled the current, finally crawling to shore on a gravel bar. Exhausted and clutching his chest, he had his first heart attack. He was transported to Bates Memorial and put into intensive care.

Dad was not expected to live, so Mother took my brother and me to see him. He was under an oxygen tent when we walked in. I slowly approached his bedside and held his hand. The oxygen tent was clear plastic and highly reflective, making it hard to see Dad's face. His forehead was beaded with sweat and his curly gray hair was moist. It was frightening to see how sick he looked. He talked very slowly and seemed very far away. Mother said he was being treated with morphine to control the pain. He told us he loved us and would be home soon.

He survived, but over the next year was never well. He would sleep for only a few hours before he would awake, gasping for air. He would get up, make a pot of coffee, retrieve his newspaper and chain-smoke Camels. Gradually his condition worsened and Dr. Rollow would frequently come to the house to do an EKG and administer a shot of morphine.

On this particular morning, Dad's chest pain was getting worse and he began to sweat. Mother asked if she should call Dr. Rollow. Dad took another nitroglycerin. Mother had poured more coffee as I sat down at the table.

Without warning, Dad slumped forward onto the tabletop, knocking over his cup. Coffee ran everywhere. His limp arms hung down beside him. He started sliding to the left and Mother tried to hold him in the chair. I joined her, but his body was too heavy for us. We eased his fall to the floor and then suddenly saw his face.

It looked black. His lips were blue and his swollen tongue protruded from his mouth. His blue eyes stared blankly at the ceiling.

"Daddy," I shouted, as Mother and I shook him. "Daddy, wake up!" No response.

I had learned the Holger-Nielsen technique during swimming lessons to revive drowning victims, so we turned Dad over on his stomach. I pushed on his back while Mother called Dr. Rollow at home. He had already left, but his wife wasn't sure whether it was for the hospital or office. Mother left messages for him at both places to call immediately. This was 1957 rural Arkansas and there were no ambulances, only hearses. An eternity passed and finally Mother called again. Meanwhile, we took turns pushing on Dad's back, trying to revive him. I thought if only the doctor would come, Dad would surely be saved.

Finally, Dr. Rollow called from his office and was on the way. Another eternity passed before he arrived. He kneeled beside Dad, felt his wrist, listened to his chest with his stethoscope, then pulled his hands into his lap and sat back on his calves. He looked up at Mother, pursed his lips and shook his head.

"He's gone."

Rage, frustration and shock welled up within me, if Dr. Rollow had only come sooner.

"Why did you take so long?" I asked indignantly.

Dr. Rollow made no reply.

"Why didn't you come sooner?" I persisted, starting to cry uncontrollably.

Mother hugged my head to her chest to quiet my outburst. There was a long silence and then Dr. Rollow spoke.

Figure 1 - Mother hugging me

"I'm sorry. There's nothing to do."

We all just sat there, staring at Dad, frozen and helpless.

Finally, Dr. Rollow called Callison McKinney Funeral Home.

"I'm at Joe Knott's home." He paused. "Joe died…another heart attack."

Dr. Rollow stayed until Carl McKinney arrived. They moved Dad onto their gurney and covered him with a blue blanket. Mr. McKinney said he would return to make "the arrangements." Dad was taken away.

Suddenly, Mom and I were alone. We stood in the kitchen, overwhelmed by emptiness and loss, trying to grasp what we had witnessed during the last hour.

We realized my older brother Joe Jr. was still asleep. We went upstairs to his room at the back of the house. I shook him. He was startled by our sudden presence and the looks on our faces.

"Dad had chest pain," I said, "another heart attack. Joe, Daddy died."

A bewildered look came over his face as he sat up rubbing his eyes, trying to determine if this was real or a dream. Then the three of us sat there crying, staring at the wall and at each other in shock and disbelief. Perhaps it would all go away. It was only nine in the morning.

When we came downstairs, I glanced at the floor where Dad had been. The kitchen would never be the same again. I went into the dining room and looked at the Fourth of July fireworks spread across the tabletop. The next day was the Fourth and Joe and I had been buying fireworks for the past three weeks, spending all the money we made mowing lawns.

They were sorted into various types: Roman candles, skyrockets, cones, fountains, sparklers, firecrackers, cherry bombs, M80s and even the punks to light them. All lined up in neat rows. Joe and I would take turns choosing the ones we wanted and then carefully put them back into rows. The Fourth of July was second only to Christmas in anticipation and excitement.

What was to become of our Fourth of July this year? You couldn't go shoot fireworks the day after your Dad died. But in truth, that was all I wanted to do and I felt guilty for having the thought. I wanted Dad's death to be over.

The word got out around town and neighbors and friends arrived with condolences and food. The kitchen became filled with hams, roasts, casseroles and pies.

Every time another person arrived I was taken back to Dad's death and my mind's attempt to block the pain was shattered. When would I be just a kid again, without this emptiness and dread?

I was sitting in a large chair in the living room when Judge Tom McGill came over.

"Don't worry, you have plenty of dads next door," he said, referring to himself and his brother-in-law, Raymond Davis. He rubbed my shoulder as I cried. "I'll miss your dad, Mike. He was a good man."

Carl McKinney, the undertaker, returned about eleven o'clock. I could hear them talking about where and when "the services" were to be held. Carl was short, had dark olive-colored skin and wore brown tinted glasses. He had a prominent forehead and eyebrows. These features made him look like a monkey. He was businesslike, completely detached from the emotions and meaning of the day. It didn't seem right.

Dad's younger brother Elmer and his family were vacationing in Florida and no one knew how to reach them. Mom said he would want to attend the funeral. Carl McKinney called the Florida Highway Patrol in Tallahassee.

"I have a death message for Mr. Elmer Knott, who is vacationing in your state. His brother has died in Arkansas." Pause. "No, we don't know where he's staying. He's driving a green Chevrolet with Oklahoma license plates."

The officer apparently expressed doubt that they could find him. Undaunted, Carl repeated, "This is a death message. He will want to be here when we bury his brother."

The first time he said "death message" I was stunned. The second time I went to my room and closed the door. His use of the term embarrassed me. I lay down on my bed, stared out the window and fell asleep. I needed an escape from the pain of it all.

When I awoke, they had decided to delay the funeral for four days to give the Highway Patrol time to find Elmer. The services were to be at the funeral home because they could seat more people. The new Presbyterian minister would officiate. Mr. Vinson had been there for only three months and hardly knew Dad, but said he would gather comments from others. Meanwhile, the Florida Highway patrol had put out an all-points-bulletin. It worked. Elmer called two days later, in tears. Mother spoke with him for a long time. He would drive straight through and be in Bentonville in time for the funeral.

That night I couldn't sleep. After an hour I went into Mom's room and found her reading the Bible. I had never seen her read the Bible. I told her I didn't understand death and asked her where Dad was now. She had been crying and simply said she didn't understand it either.

I wanted something more from Mom. I didn't know what. To make it better? To take the pain away and help me understand? I stood there beside her bed, waiting for her to comfort me. After a long silence we hugged and I went to bed and finally fell asleep.

The next morning Mother said we all had to go to the funeral home and pick out a casket for Dad. Someone had told her it was good to involve us in the funeral decisions. It was all too strange.

The second floor of the funeral home was full of open caskets. I had never seen a casket before and had only heard them referred to as coffins. They ranged in price from $1,000 to over $3,000 for the

"Guaranteed Air Tight for 50 Years" model. I stayed close to Mother. Joe seemed unaffected by this strange place and made the decisions. He thought Dad wouldn't want us to spend a lot of money for a casket. Mother agreed, so we selected the $1,350 bronze-colored Centurion. To me, the entire funeral home was unreal and frightening. It reminded me of yesterday's event, something I just wanted to forget.

That night was the Fourth of July and I had given up on any hopes of shooting off the fireworks. When we returned from the funeral home, friends were all over the house. I don't remember any of them, except for Louise Tinnin, the mother of my best friend Jimmy and one of Mother's best friends. Louise was crying and hugging me. Her large breasts and soft, fat belly engulfed me and her tears smeared my cheek as she kissed me.

"I loved Joe Knott," she shrieked in grief. "He was a great man."

The fireworks had been placed in a large white bag and stored in the walk-through closet leading to my parents' bedroom. Louise Tinnin and Mom were talking. Then Mom came over to Joe and me and said we should go to the airport road and shoot the fireworks. She felt there was no reason not to take a break from the sadness at home.

Joe and I responded with uncontrolled glee, then caught ourselves and pretended to be glum.

Finally everyone left and darkness came. We drove out to the road south of the airport and put the big bag of fireworks on the ground behind the car. The Tinnin family was there. Jimmy came up to me and said, "I'm sorry about your Dad." I nodded my head in the dark silence.

We started with the roman candles, then the skyrockets and cones. I had briefly forgotten about Dad's death until the cones. Then suddenly I remembered. I felt guilty for having fun and went over and told Mom.

"It's alright, Mike," she said. "God understands."

We fired a few more cones, then the fountains, the cherry bombs and M80s and went home.

That night I couldn't sleep, so I went upstairs to my brother's room and asked him about death. Joe just shook his head and we both cried. Crying helped and I went to bed and slept. Still, I wondered how long this cloud of sadness would last.

The next day people kept coming by, bringing food, asking questions and making their comments.

"How are you doing?"

"Be brave, little boys."

"Your father was a good man."

"He died so young."

Finally I told Mom I was going downtown to see Dad's old friend, Kester. I climbed the stairs to his woodworking shop behind my father's insurance office. The big steel door was open and Kester was sanding a wooden desk.

Kester and Dad started out selling real estate together. Dad ended up selling insurance and Kester became a handyman. His shop was huge with a high ceiling. There were stacks of wood, piles of shavings and sawdust under his table saw and hand tools on the wall above his workbench. Curls of shaved wood had accumulated on the floor from where he had planed the cherry wood for the desk. The wonderful smell of wood filled the room. My great-grandfather James Haney had built the building in the 1890s. It was constructed of brick made in the Haney brickyard west of town. I felt better just being in Kester's shop and away from all the sadness of home. As I walked in, he stopped sanding,

"Hello, Mike, how are you?"

"Okay." I could see he was sad, too.

"We lost a good man. I'll miss him."

"Kester, I don't understand death."

He just shook his head and started sanding again. He was a wonderfully simple man.

We didn't talk about Dad anymore that day. We had said all we had to say. I helped him sand the desk for two hours. As I started to leave, he said, "Mike, I was making this desk for your father."

Figure 2 - In Kester's workshop

When I arrived home, Elmer and his family had arrived. My uncle appeared exhausted by the long drive and the burden of the loss. Elmer, his wife Genevieve and Mother talked a lot that night. Joe and I listlessly played Monopoly with their two boys, Tom and Tim, but no one could enjoy the game. My cousins had just finished a long, grieving drive with their father.

Dad's oldest brother George lived in Chicago and had just had surgery on his leg to relieve an obstructed artery, so he couldn't travel. Elmer and George spoke on the phone. Everyone went to bed tired and anxious about the next day's services.

The afternoon finally came. The limousine arrived and took us to the funeral room, where we entered through a side door. We were seated in a small room with closed double doors. We sat in the front row, with the rest of the family in the rows behind us. Church hymns were playing and we could hear people beyond the closed doors.

Suddenly everything quieted, the double doors opened and there was Dad's casket. We couldn't see his face, only his chest and hands folded on his waist. There were flowers everywhere and the smell was almost sickening. We could see Mr. Vinson at the podium. He led us in prayer and then looked out into the audience behind us that we couldn't see.

"I didn't know Joe Knott for long, but long enough to know he was a good man, a good husband and a good father. I have spoken

with many of you and I know his friends and family loved Joe Knott."
He spoke with strong conviction and I began to cry.

He went on for twenty minutes and ended with another prayer.
I had partially recovered when Mr. Vinson came over, shook our hands
and said Dad was in heaven. People began filing past the casket,
holding handkerchiefs to their eyes. The sight was more than I could
stand. Mother asked that the doors be closed, but it wasn't over. We
had yet to go the cemetery.

We got back into the limousine to drive to the Bentonville
Cemetery. I had been there several times with Dad to visit the graves
of the Haneys and Knotts, but it never occurred to me that I would
one day be going there to bury him.

We waited in the limousine while they transferred the casket
onto a metal frame. Blue blankets covered a mound to the left of the
closed casket. Suddenly I realized the blankets covered dirt and the
metal frame held the casket above what would become my father's
grave. None of this seemed real.

We sat in the chairs surrounded by everyone from the funeral
home. Mr. Vinson prayed again and everyone wept. They asked Mom
if she wanted one last look, but she declined. She knew we had had
enough. They attached handles to the metal frame and the casket was
lowered into the grave. Mom stood up and threw in flowers and a
handful of dirt.

People filed by saying how much they loved Dad and how sorry they were. Joe and I began sobbing again and they escorted us to the limousine and drove us home.

Home seemed emptier than ever. Neighbors and friends came by, but I escaped to my room and closed the door. When would this pain and sadness end, so I could go back to riding my bike, playing and having fun?

***

Now, over 50 years later, I reflect back on my father's death. I have had a full, active, happy life and several children and grandchildren who give me great joy. However, I still bear the residual pain and sadness from losing my father.

My father could not be replaced, but since his death I found several men with whom I became very close, sharing the love and friendship I would have had with my father had he lived. Reflecting back, I see that my quest to form these relationships was largely subconscious. These men came into my life because I married or changed jobs or moved and had a new neighbor. I latched onto them to fill the void left by my father's death. When they passed away I was older and their deaths weren't unexpected. I wasn't devastated by their loss and have kept fond memories of them.

But I was never able to attend a conventional funeral after my father died. Some of my friends may have taken this as a sign of disrespect when they lost loved ones, but the pain was simply too great. When I explained my circumstances to them, some still believed I was being selfish. But they didn't experience what I did at age 13.

Today, instead of a funeral, some people hold a celebration of the deceased person's life. The loved one's friends and family share stories and humorous memories about the person. These are positive and uplifting ceremonies, largely devoid of the emptiness and sadness I experienced after my father's death. I think I would have much preferred that kind of goodbye.

Mother's "Mother"

Since Bentonville is in Arkansas, many people might assume it was part of the racial bigotry of the 1950s and 60s—segregation, Little Rock Central High School, federal troops and Governor Orval Faubus. Reasonable to assume, yes, but my mother taught my brother and me a different lesson about race.

The history of Oklahoma and Northwest Arkansas was dark and violent, especially the 1920s. Overt discrimination and lynching had kept our part of the state largely devoid of black inhabitants. In 1950 or '51, I remember driving with my parents to the neighboring city of Rogers, where at the city limits a rusted sign greeted all: "Nigger, Don't Let the Sun Set on You in Rogers." I queried my parents as to its meaning. My father was silent. Then my mother spoke.

"It's a bad sign and shouldn't be there."

"Mom, what do you mean 'bad'?"

"Mike, we'll talk about it later."

At that time, Bentonville had three black families. Cinco and Rabbit Dickerson was one of them. They had two boys, both married. Cinco worked at "Ma Bell," cleaning the offices housing the telephone operators and switching equipment. Seated at their switchboards, the operators would pull cords from the bottom of the switchboard and plug them into a vertical panel of holes, thereby connecting you to your neighbor or relative across town. Then they would pull a toggle switch to ring the called phone. The operator would listen until the person answered and then disconnect, unless she wasn't busy and wanted to find out the latest gossip. Cinco's job was to keep this facility clean—and spotless it was. She worked hard.

Her husband Rabbit, a small jovial man, owned Rabbit's Shoe Shine Parlor north of the square on North Main Street. Rabbit was slender and very energetic. He always wore a starched white shirt and bow tie. He knew everyone in town and greeted them all with energy and a genuine smile. If Rabbit was stymied by being black it didn't show.

His "parlor" consisted of two elevated chairs with extended metal feet. Below the seats were two drawers for polishing supplies. I loved to have my shoes shined. It felt good. Mainly, I loved Rabbit. He was nonjudgmental, simple and caring.

First, he washed each shoe with saddle soap and dried them as he spoke.

"How's your mother, Mike?"

"Okay."

"I saw your Dad yesterday at the post office. Playing Little League this year, Mike?"

"Yes, but I'm not very good at baseball."

"Do you enjoy playing?" He always sounded like he was singing when he spoke, with his near alto voice.

"Dad is so disappointed when I strike out."

We paused. "Well, Mike, it's only a game."

"I guess so, Rabbit, but people take it serious."

Rabbit's delicate hands picked up the brown tin of shoe polish from under my chair. He rubbed the polish with his bare fingers onto my shoes. This was wonderful—whatever tensions a little kid had disappeared as we spoke. Then he used a small brush to get the polish into the shoe's leather stitching and seams. Rabbit's palms were white and even the polish didn't stain them brown. I wondered why but didn't ask.

Next, he unscrewed a small bottle containing stain for the edges of the soles. He carefully brushed the sole and heels of each shoe. The volatile odor added another sensation to the experience.

Rabbit asked how my brother Joe was doing. "I don't see him much," he said.

"Joe's okay. He reads a lot."

"I see the doctors got his eyes straightened out." (My brother had been born "cross-eyed".)

"It took two operations in Fort Smith, but they got them straight."

"That's *gooood*," Rabbit said sincerely.

After the polish, he brushed each shoe while holding my foot on the metal supports. He used his right arm to brush my left shoe,

Figure 3 - Rabbit's Shoeshine Parlor

then his left arm to do my right shoe. He cleaned his brushes by pushing them together, then tossed them into the open drawer below. Then he polished my shoes with long up-and-down strokes of his rag. Placing the rag behind each shoe, he shined the heels and sides.

Finally, he dabbed his fingers into a shallow bowl of water and sprinkled a few drops on top of each shoe. Re-rolling the ends of the rag, he gave each shoe a few last rhythmic strokes, like he was working to music. This was the "spit-shine." He rubbed the insteps of each shoe with the rag and then two taps with his fingertips on the top of each shoe signaled it was over. Nearly lulled to sleep by the ritual, I didn't want it to end.

I paid him and said, "Thank you, Rabbit."

"Thank you, Mike," he replied, returning my courteous head bob.

A month after my father died, Rabbit told me how much he missed him.

"I do too, Rabbit." He knew I didn't want to talk about it. Later on, when I brought up the civil rights movement, he didn't want to talk about that either.

"Rabbit, them Cardinals are doing good."

"Yes, they is. Mike, give your mother my best. She is a fine woman, working hard to raise you two boys now that your father is gone."

So much caring and love in so few words.

"I will, Rabbit, thanks."

It was during this time in the late 1950s that racial tensions intensified. There was the Central High School crisis in Little Rock in 1957, with Governor Orval Faubus refusing school integration, followed by the arrival of federal troops. Dr. Martin Luther King, Jr. was very much in the news.

My brother and I "heard talk" at school that Dr. King was bad for trying to force integration. Many of the townspeople believed integration was wrong. We heard our schoolmates repeating what they heard from their parents, that forcing integration was evil and Dr. King was a bad person.

Initially, Mother listened in silence as Joe and I reported what our classmates said. Then one evening, after repeating what we had heard at school—"Niggers were bad, Martin Luther King was bad, nigger-this and nigger-that"—her silence ended.

My mother was a woman of few words, allowing Joe and me to find our own way even when she knew we were misguided. That evening in the kitchen she put down her chopping knife, rinsed and dried her hands on her apron, removed it and laid it on the kitchen counter and motioned us into the living room. Mother had something to say and Joe and I sat in silence and listened.

"Joe, Mike, what you are hearing is not true. Black people are good people, just as good and smart as you and me." There was a resolute quality to her voice. "Cinco and Rabbit are good people and you like them, don't you?"

"Yes, Mother."

"They work hard and have good children, don't they?"

"Yes, Mother."

"Then don't listen to people who say things that you know aren't true."

"Yes, Mother."

Mom was shy and tended not to look directly at you when she spoke, but that was not the case that day. She looked directly into our eyes, observing our faces for any sign that we didn't fully believe or understand what she had said. She didn't find any such sign.

In the years that followed, I can remember only one other time when Mother made a similar plea. When my father was alive he participated in the "Negro Minstrels." Mother, Joe and I attended his performance in the Bentonville High School auditorium.

The "Minstrels" had been an annual event for years, though we only went this one time. Local white men came on stage and sat in the wings. They wore black makeup, red lipstick, straw hats and white shoes. A piano played ragtime music and the men sang. Then the piano and singing stopped and someone told a joke inferring that blacks were ignorant or irresponsible. Mother stood up, firmly grasped Joe and me by the wrists (not by our hands, as usual) and we exited the auditorium. She said nothing and I heard nothing more on the subject.

A few weeks later, I asked Rabbit to help me understand.

"Well, Mike, she made a statement."

"Mother didn't *say* anything, Rabbit."

"Yes she did."

I don't believe my father was a racist. I think he simply followed the crowd by participating in the community's annual event until Mother put an end to it. My father identified far too much with his poor Irish stonemason ancestors to be a bigot. However, even following the crowd was not okay with Mother. She had very strong feelings about this issue. I wondered why.

As I grew into adolescence, I realized my mother was different from her own mother. My mother was not a bigot and her actions and words proved it. But my grandmother Mammaw was a down-to-the-bone bigot. The difference between these two women tells quite a story.

Mammaw called black people "niggers" and spoke the word with the conviction of profound bigotry and racial hatred. During my youth I would cringe whenever I heard the word.

"Mammaw, that's not good to say."

"I don't care. I hate them."

"Please, just say blacks."

She compromised. "Okay, niggras."

She never changed but lived to wish she had later.

Mammaw was born in 1885 in Port Arthur, Texas. This was a near-coastal town in southeastern Texas, just across the Sabine River from Louisiana. Unlike Northwest Arkansas, this was the "true South." Raised in a well-to-do family, she was a pampered Southern belle of the time. There was a family picture of *her* mother dressed in the finery of the times, a formal, unsmiling pose that stated, "I am the stuff."

To clarify, I am discussing three generations. Mammaw was born in 1885, so her mother (my great-grandmother) probably gave birth to her while she was in her early twenties, placing my great-grandma's birth in the early 1860s.

The Civil War ended in 1865, but, to be sure, most Southerners were not happy with the outcome of "the Waaar" and their attitudes toward the "Negroes" hadn't changed. Slavery and racism had become illegal in the law of the land, but not in the minds and actions of most Southerners. I must be fair to my grandmother and great-grandmother, because these were huge changes for society to accept and that acceptance came slowly.

Therefore, my grandmother Mammaw was no different from her mother with regard to racial sentiments, but *my* mother was completely different from her mother. This change between three generations was not gradual or incremental in any way. The change from Mammaw to my mother was absolute; a complete 180-degree change in how these two women viewed the black race. Again, I wondered why.

In her seventies and eighties, Mammaw developed senility or Alzheimer's disease. My mother found it impossible to care for her and she went to a nursing home. During her last 15 years she was overcome by profound paranoia. She lived in constant fear and terror that her black nurses and aides were stealing her money (she had none) and clothes. The doctors tried numerous medications to calm her, but to no avail. It was obvious that her paranoia was as real to her as the light of day. Wracked by agitation and sometimes terror, she couldn't sleep. When I visited her at the nursing home I apologized to the staff, most of whom were black, for Mammaw's offensive comments. They at least said they understood.

Her final years were ironic, given her deep, paranoid hatred of the black race. She had hurt many people, but in the end caused herself the most pain. Her hatred ended up tormenting her and it was not a pretty sight. In the end, hatred hurts the one who hates.

So, to return to the question: why was my mother the exact opposite of Mammaw with regard to race? Years later, I still had no answer to this question.

A long time after Mammaw had mercifully passed away, my mother was living in Bella Vista, Arkansas. Before she became blind from macular degeneration, she labeled all of the old family pictures.

During this time I remembered her mentioning having had a nanny as a baby.

My mother, Theron Mae, had a sister who was two years older named Mary Elizabeth. In one family photograph, two black women were each holding a small child. Because Mother was blind at this time, I described the photograph. Suddenly, Mother smiled warmly and her eyes teared.

"That was my mother," she said, choking up on the last word.

Knowing Mammaw as I did, I was sure she never changed a diaper on her girls. She loved her children, but she wasn't the loving, holding, nurturing mother type. I'm sure that when my infant mother cried out at night, it was Ruth, her black nanny, who got up, held her and lovingly rocked her back to sleep.

So, when Joe and I came home from school and started talking about "nigger-this" and "nigger-that," we were talking about my mother's "mother." She had no tolerance for our derogatory talk of the black race. Two small boys were taught by their mother to love and respect all.

Ruth's memory had lived on inside my mother and now the love from both of them live on inside my brother and me.

Robert "Kester" Evans (1900-1997)

Of all the Bentonville folks I knew in the 1950s, Kester Evans was the most interesting and novel. Nearly all the locals knew him because he played the saw, which he stroked with a bass bow to make wonderful melodic tones. He played at schools, churches and for me and was always quite a hit. He said he knew about 150 songs.

However, there was much more to Kester that amused and entertained me. He was a master storyteller and I loved to listen. He became family to me after my father died.

Kester moved to Bentonville when he was nearly 40 years old and lived another 56 years. However, he had an interesting eventful life before coming to Bentonville.

Born in southeastern Kansas in Rantoul, a rural town of 200, his parents "drew" a claim in the Oklahoma Land Lottery. So in August 1901 the whole family left Kansas in a covered wagon. Kester was an infant and nearly froze to death during the family's meandering route to Lawton, Oklahoma. Oklahoma Land Rushes were historically fraught with violence, but the lottery of 1901 allowed a family to stake their claim to a 160-acre homestead in a much more orderly manner.

Kester's family lived there for the three years required to make good on their claim and then sold the farm and moved to Stillwater, Oklahoma. Kester didn't remember why they moved, but remembered the covered wagon trip to the new farm with a single word: "Rough."

Figure 4 - Kester telling me stories

Kester loved horses and at age 5 rode bareback on a pony. He loved to sleep in the "mangers" with the horses. By age 8 he drove a large water wagon and could plow with a small walking plow pulled by two horses.

"I could barely turn the plow around at the end of the row," he told me, but what he lacked in size he made up for by "getting the horses to help."

Kester said he "learned everything there was to know about horses," but when he was 19 he saw his first automobile. He was in his fifties when he told me of his love for horses, but I could hear the emotion he still felt for the loss of that way of life.

Work is what Kester remembered most during his early years. His family grew cotton on a rented 40-acre farm. They had no radio, electricity, or indoor plumbing. He said they didn't play games and had "no pleasures." They awoke at sunrise, ate breakfast, worked all day, came home, ate supper and went to bed—six days a week. Kester only went to school for one full term and that was because the hail ruined the cotton crop and he didn't have to pick it. He said he learned a lot during that one full term, but didn't attend any school past the eighth grade because he had to work to help the family. This is partially explained by the fact that his father was 53 years old when he was born.

When Kester was just 8, his father was in his early 60s farming 40 acres of cotton and needed all the help he could get to support the family. Kester did what was needed, but it took the fun of his youth away.

"We would go to church on Sunday and then in Sunday school they'd have what they called 'literary,'" he told me. "Kids would learn to make a speech and then they'd have a little comedy in it, you know."

"Did you do that?" I asked.

"Yeah, I remember one speech that went like this." And then Kester recited for me:

Gee, I'm glad I'm not a girl,
Hands to hold and hair to curl.
Skirts flippin' around their knees,
Can't do nothin' like you please.
Can't whistle, fart, or swim,
Just fold your hands and sit up prim.
Grandpa says it's just a chance,
That we got to wearin' pants.
Says that when kids were small,
They put dresses on them all.

Kester said the preachin' in church was "hell fire and brimstone," and it was considered a disgrace to go to the picture show.

Figure 5 - Kester on horseback

Work was Kester's youth and in 1915, at age 15, intending to run away from home, he rode his saddle horse from his home in Stillwater to work on his uncle's wheat farm in southern Kansas. During the three-day trip he slept on hay in farmers' barns. Once a farmer checked his pockets for matches but let him stay. The hay kept him warm during the cold nights, but made him itch the rest of the trip.

In Kansas he drove a four-horse gangplow cultivating the wheat fields. After several weeks of work, he returned home. Because of heavy rain, the Arkansas River was very high where it joined the Chikaskia River. He headed his mount into the river, slid off its back and held onto the horse's tail as it swam across the high waters.

"It was scary, but I had to cross. I had to do somethin'."

Kester was one month and one day too young to be drafted into World War I. Four of his half-brothers were drafted and one was killed in France. I asked him what he remembered about the 1918-19 influenza epidemic.

"I caught the flu in Kansas before I left for home and slept in a barber shop for two weeks with a 103.5 degree fever the entire time. That's when they died like flies…stacked 'em up like cord wood."

He started an apprenticeship in the carpenters union in Stillwater and "put in a year and a half. Then I heard they needed a thousand carpenters in L.A." When Kester arrived in Los Angeles, it turned out to be a real estate scheme. He was 23 years old.

Figure 6 - Kester crossing the Arkansas River

While there, he did any kind of work he could get, including "cleaning roots out of sewer lines and digging graves at Odd Fellows Cemetery. It was hard work."

He finally got a job selling auto polish and accessories. He filled a Model T Ford with auto polish and drove straight through to San Francisco. He stayed in a "roomin' house" ("Many of these were whorehouses, but not this one") on 8th Street off Market Street, south of the Ferry Building, which was under construction at the time.

Kester asked me, "Is the Ferry Building done yet?"

I told him yes. I was interviewing him in 1980 and it had been completed 56 years before. Kester had been curious about that for a long time.

Before he left for California in 1920, a fellow carpenter in Oklahoma showed Kester how to make a sound on the saw and he taught himself to play. He bought a Czechoslovakian horsehair bass bow in L.A., played in various places and won several amateur contests.

He left San Francisco and drove to Tacoma, Washington. During this time his G & G Auto Polish bosses weren't treating him fairly, so he gave up the car and headed back to Oklahoma by hitching rides on freight trains. Kester had mastered "riding the rails" and was never thrown off by the conductors. On one train he noticed a "hot box" and alerted the conductors, who stopped the train, fixed the problem and showed their appreciation by letting Kester stay on. The "hot box" could have caused a wheel or axle to fail, resulting in a derailment.

Kester told me he had a special technique for jumping off a slow moving train without injuring himself. He said he doubled up, jumped and landed running "without going ass over tea kettle" like others did, ending up with deep scratches on their hands and faces or even worse. However, one time his technique didn't work and he ended up scratching his hands and knees.

He traveled through California and Washington, then back home and on to Chicago and the East Coast. During his travels he played the saw in numerous amateur contests and taverns. He said he always moved on to the next town with more money than he had arrived with. Kester was "a ramblin' man" and enjoyed traveling and meeting new people. In addition to the saw, he became proficient at twelve other "novelty instruments," as he called them. He made a putty knife chirp like a bird and played a tune on eight metal goblets of varying sizes by hitting them with a wooden mallet.

Kester bought a pair of "Swiss Bells" in L.A. They are correctly called "Four-in-a-Hand" bells. R.H. Mayland in Brooklyn, New York made Kester's bells. I have seen no reference to "Swiss Bells," but this added a special mystery to Kester's stories when I was just a young boy.

To understand how they are played, I must first focus on a single bell and how it's made and positioned. The clapper is hinged at the center but only swings in a single fixed direction, not back and forth like regular bells. The four bells are mounted on a metal base and are equidistant from a center point. A wooden handle is attached at this center point. During play, the handles are held so the bells point up, one set in each hand. One set has notes C, E, D and F and the other set has notes C, A, B and G.

Kester was the only person I ever saw play the "Swiss Bells." Very few people play them today, perhaps because it's a difficult instrument. They require the integrated movement of hands, wrists and arms, as well as intense concentration on the tunes played. Playing a note requires "loading" the correct bell, or positioning of the bell *before* play, then moving that bell to play the note. At the same time that note is being played, the next bell has to be positioned to be played, whether on the other set or by quickly repositioning the same set to play a different note. In addition, each set of bells is around five pounds, making them heavy to hold and play. Combine all this with the fact that the bells only play the single note of a song.

Kester was completely self-taught and played by holding the bells near his shoulders. By twisting his wrists, he would "load" the bell and then move the set away from his shoulders, forward and down, to play the note. I saw a video of a man playing the bells by holding them away from his body, then moving the set North, South, East, or West to play. This latter technique seemed more efficient, allowing for faster play.

Kester was 27 when he returned to Oklahoma from his West and East Coast travels. He took any job he could find, but his random pursuits led him to a job that nearly cost him his life. He was working for a "gasage company," equivalent to today's bulk gasoline supplier. His boss had installed an underground gasoline storage tank, 20 feet long and 10 feet in diameter. The inside of the tank needed painting, but first it had to dry out.

Kester was resourceful and suggested heating the inside of the tank by burning natural gas inside it. His boss approved the plan. Kester and his coworkers ran a gas line inside the tank and constructed a burner to mix air and gas. The plan was to let it burn all night to dry out the tank and then they would paint it the next day.

With the flame lit, the access door to the tank was left open to allow air to enter. However, that night, unknown to Kester, a coworker saw light coming from inside the tank and closed the access door. Although the flame went out when the air supply was cut off, natural gas continued to flow into and fill the tank.

The next day Kester arrived to find the burner was out. (This was 1928, before natural gas was "odorized" by adding the distinctive rotten egg smell we all know today. Natural gas has nearly no odor in its natural state. It was odorized only after a 1937 school explosion in London, Texas that killed 300 students and teachers!)

Kester descended into the tank via a ladder. In so doing, he introduced air into the gas mixture and then added the final needed ingredient by striking a match to relight the flame.

The tank instantly exploded, blowing the ladder, gas line and burner clear through the access door. Kester's clothes burst into flame. It was a cool day and he was wearing a wool shirt and heavy underclothes. The explosion burned them completely off.

City officials inspected the tank the next day. It had been constructed of one-quarter inch thick steel, overlapping at the edges and secured with three-quarter inch diameter rivets. The explosion tore the rivets out of the steel in several places, rupturing the tank.

If the explosion could rip rivets out of steel plates, you can imagine what it did to Kester. Both eardrums were permanently ruptured and never healed. The outer edges of both ears were burned off, making them shorter and pointy and resulting in a pixie look. He had worn gloves that day, but had removed the left one to light the match. His left hand was permanently scarred; his tendons so damaged that he couldn't fully extend his fingers. Kester thought the injury allowed him to play the saw better.

Kester was hospitalized for three months, sustaining burns on 30% of his body. Burn care at the time wasn't as advanced as it is now and the doctors didn't think he would live. But he was young and strong and recovered, although for the rest of his life he wore hearing aids.

I saw clear flaws in Kester's logic about burning natural gas inside a gasoline storage tank. However, given what happened to him, I never brought this up.

Kester received no permanent disability from the company, state, or federal government. The famous quote by Teddy Roosevelt fit his situation: "Do what you can, with what you've got, where you are." If he hadn't heard the quote, he certainly lived it. There was even a humorous result from the loss of his eardrums. Kester smoked cigarettes for a time and would bet people he could blow smoke from both ears. I saw him win several bets. In his later years he quit doing this out of fear he might damage his hearing even more.

After a long recovery, Kester moved to Bentonville from Stillwater, Oklahoma because the air and water were better, but he also told me, "I just felt better over here." He probably wanted a fresh start away from his near death experience, but we never discussed it. Kester taught me to leave the past behind, remember the good times and look forward to a better future.

After arriving in Bentonville he did real estate sales and got his broker's license, but didn't do well and by the time I met him in the 1950s he was working as a handyman.

My dad let Kester put his shop in a building he owned in downtown Bentonville, rent-free. If he wasn't out on a fix-it job, he was in his shop. I would go there after school. The shop had a wonderful aroma of oak, cherry and cedar, of sawdust and wood shavings. If he wasn't working on a job, he'd be tinkering with new gadgets.

He never married, probably because of his disfigurement, but it didn't seem to bother him. He liked to say, "I'm the way I is." I believe Kester expressed a lot in those few words. He was like my mother in his view of life. They both had experienced very hard times and personal tragedies, but neither dwelled on the past. They accepted where and who they were at any given time. If more bad times came their way, they went forward, unimpeded by the past and remaining optimistic that things would get better.

Dad always invited Kester and Mutt Morgan, a local electrician, for Thanksgiving and Christmas dinner. Neither of them had families, so they joined ours. Kester always brought his magic with him, so I was the big winner. He had a large cloth sack containing all of his novelty instruments. After we ate he played for an hour, starting with the saw for several tunes, then the putty knife and silver goblets. Then he and Mutt would walk the two blocks to downtown. Kester lived behind my dad's insurance office and Mutt above the pool hall. Both were bachelors.

Kester generated almost as much excitement for me as opening Christmas presents. He was magic to me, I loved him and we were to get even closer after my father had died and I spent even more time with him. He and my dad were longtime friends and "bent a few elbows together." We both missed my father but shared the loss in silence; Dad was gone and talk wouldn't bring him back.

Kester worked in the maintenance department of St. Mary's Hospital in Rogers, Arkansas after I graduated from high school in 1962 and started college. He worked there until 1972, when they required that he retire and start receiving Social Security. Kester was happy working at the hospital. He expressed surprise that Social Security sent him so much money every month, "I could never spend it all," he told me, "but they keep sending it." He showed me his bank account statement a few years before he died and he had almost $100,000.

I lived away from Bentonville after college, but returned frequently to see my mother and always spent time with Kester during each visit. In his later years he read Westerns and watched television. He owned a little house on West Easy Street in Rogers. He didn't pay much for it because it was only 300 feet from the railroad tracks, but that didn't bother Kester because he was deaf. He developed bladder cancer and survived the surgery, but died suddenly in the hospital of a heart attack or blood clot. The nurses called me the night he died. I was the closest thing to family he had and he was family to me.

I flew home and made the burial arrangements, ordered the headstone and got permission to bury him in my family's older cemetery area with the first generation Haneys. On his headstone I added Kester's standard farewell remark to me: "Happy Landing."

I'm not sure what he meant by the phrase. Kester never flew in an airplane, but I think "Happy Landing" meant for us to be who we are, wherever we are, the way he accepted himself and his life, "The way I is."

My Irish Family History

Much of my family's history was passed down to my generation through word-of-mouth from our parents. The Haneys were our family's link to Ireland. We held their memory dear and for good reason. We were proud of my great-grandfather, James Haney, who survived difficult conditions in leaving Ireland for England and who eventually arrived in America to prosper in a new life.

James' parents, Thomas and Mary Haney, had seven children when they left Ireland in 1845 and journeyed to Middleton, Lancashire, England (near Manchester). They left to escape "The Great Hunger," which caused 1.5 million Irish to starve to death during the famine of 1845-1849. Had they stayed, it is likely our Irish linage would have been buried in a pauper's grave in County Offaly, Ireland (known then as King's County).

Thomas Haney, born in 1807, could remember prior famines, specifically 1817, 1821-1822 and 1830-1834. He married Mary Madden, born in 1819 and they eventually had nine children. Thomas had been a farmer in Ireland and it's possible that he worked in England during the previous harvests like many other Irishmen. They would plant the potatoes in the spring and he would leave the family for the summer and make money in England.

Thomas was poor and his family had a subsistence living. He chose to immigrate to England and not America because many Irish escaped starvation in Ireland only to die aboard "coffin ships" bound for the U.S.   This was the first of the Haney decisions that was incredibly well-timed.   The crop failure the following year was complete throughout Ireland. As the mass exodus accelerated, British ports eventually closed and shiploads of Irish immigrants were forced to return. Thomas Haney made it to England just in time.   In his book *The Great Famine 1845-51*, John Percival writes, "Huge numbers took ships to across the Irish Sea to Liverpool and many hundreds died there." Thomas and Mary had the good sense to move further south, near Manchester, their second timely decision.   Thomas Haney remained a farmer in England until he died.

The English have been widely condemned for not helping the starving Irish more. At the time, the English strongly believed that market forces and time would resolve the problem. The famine was seen as nature's and God's way of dealing with the problem of overpopulation. However, there was much more to this story than economics.

In *The Great Famine 1845-51*, Percival writes: "[T]he bare truth was that the English regarded Ireland as a colony, useful as a supplier of food, but full of idle, turbulent and racially inferior people, who might be helped a little if the need arose, but not at too great a cost." Others believed that the Irish were hard working, oversexed and liked to drink. (I agree with these "others.") If they survived the journey to

England, the Irish were regarded as less than human beings— insignificant slaves fit for nothing but cutting wood and drawing water.

In the final analysis, the Irish dependence on the potato was so great that starvation was inevitable; however, the English could have done more to save lives.

James, the third son of Thomas and Mary Haney and my great-grandfather, was born May 4, 1837, so he was eight years old when the family immigrated to England. At thirteen, he went to work as an errand boy in a cotton mill. After a short time he was put to spinning cotton, but this wasn't to his liking. After a year and half he left to work in the brick, stone and carpenter's trade for three and a half years as an apprentice and then ran away.

After a year he returned, was arrested and given the choice of returning to his trade or jail. He chose the former, worked for three and a half years more, joined the Trades and Benevolent Union in Manchester and served in every capacity. He became bank trustee of the society in 1860.

James was 22 years old when he married Mary Adams, age 20, in Middleton, England in 1859. My great-grandmother Mary was born May 21, 1840 in County Mayo, Ireland and was described as a "small woman with red hair." The Adams' family immigration from County Mayo to England would probably have been even more difficult, since that county was the worst hit by the famine.

James was 28 when he left England for America in 1865. One year later, Mary joined James in the U.S. with their two sons. Conditions in America had improved and James and Mary no doubt had some means when they left England. Most importantly, the brick, stone and carpenter's trade would serve James very well in America and in the city of Bentonville.

New York City, their point of arrival, didn't look much like the Ireland they sought, so James and Mary Haney kept moving west. They lived in various states and then settled in St. Louis where James worked his trade. In 1869 they went overland on the Old Wire Road to Springfield, Missouri and in 1871 settled in Bentonville. The Ozark Mountains of northwest Arkansas looked like the "rolling emerald green hills" of their beloved Ireland, or at least that's what my father told me one night with tears in his eyes.

James Haney established a brickyard west of Bentonville. Over the next thirty years, he made bricks and constructed many of the buildings in downtown Bentonville that still stand today.

James and Mary Adams together had ten children: John (1862), Eliza (1864), Tom (1866), William (1872), Charles (1874), George (1875), my grandmother Kate (1878), Ada (1880) and James A. (1883). Nine of these children survived the common childhood diseases, a remarkable occurrence in the late 19th century. Mary was 43 when she had her last child, James A., the namesake of his father.

The Haneys were good Irish Catholics when they came to the U.S., but the generations to follow were Presbyterian. One night my father told my brother and me the story of their conversion after he had a few drinks (and, once again, with tears in his eyes). Dad considered himself Irish through-and-through, never mentioning that the name Knott was most likely English.

Dad had all the Irish characteristics—love of work, talk, drink and music and was seriously superstitious.

He told us there was no Catholic church in northwest Arkansas when the Haneys settled in Bentonville. So they apparently decided to take a break from religion and concentrated on making bricks and building the downtown.

That was okay with everyone, except the Ku Klux Klan. They had heard the Haneys were Catholic and to them it was a strange religion practiced by foreigners. They apparently thought my ancestors were planning to overthrow the local church. So the KKK paid a late night visit to their home and burned a cross in their front yard. James Haney came out on the front porch, recognized most of the Klansmen and told them to go home.

Whether it was the KKK or James' belief that it was time for the family to return to spiritual ways, the Haney family turned up in the Presbyterian church the following Sunday. They baptized the little ones and all signed on as new members. Everyone was happy. The

Figure 7 - James Haney and the KKK

Haneys' religious conversion had gone smoothly and the grass grew back in their front yard. James had apparently caved in to the Klansmen, but at the same time his willingness to be flexible and adaptable allowed the Irish to integrate into Bentonville's culture. Flexibility and adaptability were the essential attributes that allowed the Irish to prosper in this country and, specifically, for the Haneys to prosper in Bentonville. To the end of his life James still considered himself a Catholic, so the "conversion" was more of a business decision than a religious one.

Life for the Haney family was good in the 1880s and 1890s. James had a large family and a successful brickyard and construction business in his new country. At this time the Haney family children ranged in age from nine to 30. James Haney was 55.

In 1888, William, the fourth child was accepted to West Point at age 22. This must have been a time of great joy for James and Mary. They began their lives in abject poverty and now their son was leaving for West Point. I can visualize the farewell dinner for William, with James at the head of the table, his wife Mary at the opposite end and their nine children at their sides. Eleven people celebrating life in America. Alas, unknown to them that night, their Irish luck was running out.

Following graduation from West Point in 1892, William returned to Bentonville on leave, before proceeding to his first assignment with the 8th Army at Fort Niobrara, Kansas and then field duty near Lima, Montana. He was unaware he had contracted tuberculosis while at West Point and he managed to serve for three years before he became too sick and was given an honorable medical discharge. He returned home to Bentonville to die, but before he did infected several members of his family. William, Eliza, George and their father, James Haney, died over the next five years. John and James Jr. died a few years later. Mary Adams Haney buried her husband and five children over a period of ten years.

Kate, Ada, Charles and Tom F. all lived into their late 60s and 70s. Kate, the third from the youngest and my grandmother, was the only child of the original ten to ever marry and have children. She married Elmer Conway Knott and had three boys: George, Joseph (my father) and Elmer Jr. They lived in the Haney home built with Haney brick on South Main Street in Bentonville. Rheumatic fever killed Elmer Knott in 1916, less than a year after his last son was born.

Kate's sister, my father's Aunt Ada, lived in the Haney house and her surviving brothers Charles and Tom F. lived directly behind them in a small white house. Charles wrote poetry and Tom sold real estate. My mother would only say that "Tom was a rounder" with many girlfriends, while Charles "was different." He might have been gay and tried to enter the priesthood. They all ate at the Haney house, where Mama Kate and Aunt Ada raised the boys.

Aunt Ada worked at the Bank of Bentonville and started saving money for my father and his two brothers to go to college. As time went on the entire family gave her money for the boys' college fund, which eventually amounted to $10,000 for each of them! Joseph and Elmer graduated from the University of Arkansas at Fayetteville and George from the University of Missouri School of Journalism in Columbia. George moved to Chicago and became an advertising executive and journalist. Elmer moved to Oklahoma City and was an executive with Amoco Oil. My father Joseph initially moved to Washington, D.C. and worked in the administration of the U.S. Capitol Police, but didn't like being away from Bentonville. In less than a year he returned home to eventually marry my mother and sell insurance.

Mary Adams Haney, the small Irish woman with red hair, lived until 1923 and the age of 83. Four of her ten children survived her.

***

Every family has similar stories, some with greater hardship and others with less, but looking back at the Haneys' story several decisions stand out. Obviously, Thomas Haney's timely departure from Ireland allowed the family to survive "The Great Famine." Second, James Haney's departure from England and his success in America are a pivotal part of our family's history. Third, Aunt Ada's college fund and the contributions from other Haney children were responsible for moving the Haney/Knott children up a notch on the socioeconomic ladder.

Over a period of about sixty years, the family survived absolute poverty and certain starvation to flourish in America. Thank you, Thomas, James and all the other James Haney children. We now have you within us! Remembering you is your immortality. That is why I have written this story.

Sophie Dickson Knott: A Life in Black and Red

While we were related, my interest in Sophie Knott wasn't due to family ties but rather to the mysterious tragedies of life. Sophie's first child, Jimmy, was run over and killed by a car at age eight. Her second child, Dickson, was killed in World War II in 1944. Her husband died six years later, leaving her alone and sharing ownership of the Eagle Milling Company with Gordon Knott, the only surviving son of E. P. "Bud" Knott, Sophie's brother-in-law and my future stepfather. Gordon's only sibling was also killed in World War II.

It's hard to imagine the despair she must have felt over these losses. The only good news was that Eagle Milling was a successful feed mill and supplier of chicken feed to numerous farmers in northwest Arkansas. It was well managed by Gordon, so he and Sophie shared good profits. Sophie didn't have business skills and her "work" for the company consisted of signing checks on Wednesday afternoons. Her shiny black Lincoln Continental was parked next to the bulk feed delivery trucks every Wednesday afternoon. After Sophie's husband died in 1950, she dressed in mourning for years, the custom of the time. She would emerge from the Lincoln dressed in black and wearing a large black hat with a veil, to make her way into the company office.

Figure 8 - Sophia outside Eagle Milling Co.

Sophie had a high-pitched, shy-sounding voice with a trill of a warble that didn't sit well after a brief hello. When we spoke, I was never quite sure if she didn't hear me or was preoccupied, because she usually ignored me and carried on with her own conversation. But I was just a kid and kids back then respected almost all adults. While Sophie spoke, I obeyed the "seen and not heard" expectation of my parents.

Sophie gradually emerged from mourning and her zest and spirit for life returned. She added lace to her wardrobe, wore larger and more elaborate hats (with the veil ever present) and sported a bouffant hairstyle.

She developed a liking for New Orleans and specifically the French Quarter. Each spring Gordon transported Sophie, her two large steamer chests and several hatboxes to the train station in Rogers, Arkansas, seven miles from Bentonville. There was now another major change in her wardrobe, as she began wearing stylish red dresses and hats without a veil for the trip south. She was excited about the New Orleans seafood and Cajun cuisine. The mourning was over as the "red Sophie" put her tragedies and losses behind.

No one knew her activities in New Orleans, but the word around town was that Sophie had a "gigolo" in New Orleans. I asked my mother what that meant and she said we would talk about it later.

If Sophie had a male acquaintance, why couldn't he just be someone she was dating? I suppose paying a man for "services" made for much better gossip in a rural, 1950s town. Perhaps Sophie's high-pitched voice, new car and fancy clothes didn't sit well with some of the locals.

After Sophie's return from New Orleans, the "black Sophie" sometimes returned. But in 1955, a new, bright red Thunderbird convertible appeared in Sophie's driveway. She didn't drive it much in Bentonville, as there wasn't enough head clearance in the car for her enormous hats. She also complained about all the bruises she sustained getting into and out of the driver's seat.

I was 10 years old and my love for cars was surging. The Thunderbird was America's sports car (besides the Corvette, but I had never seen one of those). Sophie was family, but she never took me for a ride.

Soon it became clear why she had purchased the car. "Red Sophie" needed a car to drive while in New Orleans (or for her "gigolo" to drive, as the gossips said). Since New Orleans was too far a drive for Sophie, this required special arrangements. Bennie McCool, one of Gordon's employees, drove the car to the city prior to Sophie's arrival by train. However, Bennie's wife required certain rules to be followed—Bennie had to deliver the car and be back in Bentonville *before* Sophie departed for New Orleans. The rules were reversed with the summer retrieval of her car. Bennie was probably the only person who knew any details about Sophie's activities in New Orleans, but if so, he wasn't talking.

Sophie had found some happiness to make up for the tragedies and losses of her earlier life. Gradually, however, she spent less time in New Orleans and finally settled into her small red brick home on North Main Street. She never would disclose her age and her passing added to her mystique. Her tombstone reads:

"Sophie Dickson Knott ? - 1975."

Chapter Two

Neighborhood

Ralph and Rose

I knew everyone in my neighborhood. My playmate then and still my oldest and closest friend today, was Jimmy Tinnin. We lived across West Central Avenue from each other. Another playmate, Bill Davis, lived next door. His dad owned Oklahoma Tire and Supply. Leda Bryant, my father's secretary at the insurance agency, lived two doors down to the west with her sister Cecil.

Ida Tinnin (Jimmy's grandmother) served as the Bentonville School Superintendent and was known for integrating the entire school system in one day, when Ron Stewart entered the fourth grade. Ron was the only black child of school age in Bentonville in 1954 when the Supreme Court found that segregation was unconstitutional. Ida said it was best for him and would save the school district any home schooling costs. It was a non-event, as Ron had few problems, graduated from high school and then worked in nearby Rogers after graduation. This is an ironic occurrence, given that at the time Rogers had no black residents, at least partly because of signs outside the city limits that stated, "Nigger, don't let the sun set on you in Rogers."

At that time, my future stepfather, Gordon, lived three doors down with his wife Josephine. After my father and Josephine both died, my mother and Gordon married each other. Gordon was also a Knott, but the fork in the family tree occurred many generations back. Still, it was very confusing how Mother remarried and kept the same last name. Gordon was very cosmopolitan, considering the rural isolation of Bentonville. He grew orchids and exotic plants in the greenhouse behind his garage. Gordon and my mother enjoyed many good years together before he died in his mid-60s of cancer. Mother had bad luck picking men.

I knew many of our other neighbors as well. Some were elderly or didn't have much interest in a curious little kid. Included among them were Ralph and his wife, who lived across West Central Avenue and Rose, who lived next door to Ralph. A gravel alley separated their properties. Both ran small businesses. Ralph's Electric Motor Rewinding and Repair Shop was located at the rear of his property, while Rose's Gift Shop was in the front of hers. The sidewalks on both sides of West Central Avenue were set back from the curb, creating a grassy strip planted with redbud trees every fifty feet from downtown to the future Highway 71 bypass location. In addition, large mature trees hung over the street. In the springtime, they formed a tunnel lined with pink blossoms, a small-town delight. West Central Avenue was dubbed the "Silk Stocking Row" of Bentonville.

Ralph's business entailed fixing and selling electrical motors and parts. He emerged from his house only to mow his lawn and trim the grass along his sidewalk. In fact, Ralph was the only person in town who bothered with trimming that way. His driveway was also somewhat unique. The gravel was of uniform size and neatly contained by concrete edging. No loose gravel anywhere, no grass or weeds growing near the edges like others in the neighborhood. His house, garage and shop were gray. The house and garage were a softer tone of gray, but the shop was Navy gray, indicating his World War II service.

Although I didn't realize it at the time, all of this gave me my first clues into Ralph's personality.

I had explored all of Bentonville's various shops—welding shops, machine shops, woodworking shops, muffler shops, body and radiator repair shops, gun shops, shoe repair shops, appliance repair shops and lawnmower repair shops. There were no television repair shops because TV did not yet exist in the Bentonville of the early 50s. My father was a friendly man, known and liked by everyone in town. I was Joe's son and because of him everyone knew who I was when I walked in and tolerated my questions about what I saw.

Summer days gave me a lot of time to fill. This mandated new territory to explore and because Ralph and Rose were just across the street and both had businesses, boredom enticed me to wander into their spaces. They shared one thing—neither liked a curious little kid walking into their space. But they were very different in how they expressed their dislike for my intrusions.

One day I quietly entered Ralph's shop without him noticing me. I stood there in wonder and awe. Not only were the shop's walls and ceilings painted Navy gray, but also the floors. I had never seen anyone paint their shop floors. Everything was spotless. No drips or smell of oil, no grease smudges, no sawdust, no metal turnings, not even a swept up pile of trash awaiting pickup. Four large steel tables with welded steel legs filled the center of the room. Surrounding the tables were numerous machines—a table saw, drill press, grinders, a lathe and several others unknown to me. Tall stainless steel toolboxes with numerous drawers stood in close proximity.

This was a special place—Ralph's space. It was like no other I had ever seen. I felt out of place just standing there.

Ralph was dressed in dark gray matching work clothes—clean, ironed, maybe even starched. He wore an equally neat leather apron tied in back.

The steel tables were exactly the same size and equally spaced from each other, covered with electrical motors and parts of all types and sizes. The motors and parts were aligned in perfectly straight rows, like military troops ready for inspection. Any wires protruding from the items curled into uniform circles.

Ralph sat facing the wall with an apparatus that held an electrical motor, surrounded by several spools of shiny wires that fed into the motor's center. As soon as he noticed me, the rewinding stopped. Turning his head, he made no verbal greeting but simply stared. Two bright lights attached to the wall above silhouetted his profile. I was not welcome. However, I couldn't resist picking up a few parts from the tables. I was thrusting daggers into his soul with each touch. Watching my every move, his jaw quivered and lips pursed. He never spoke a word, but made mental notes of everything I touched so he could restore order when I left.

"It's getting late, I better go home for supper," I said, even though it was only four in the afternoon. I wanted to return to Ralph's shop, to understand and learn more about him, but I never went back after I saw his agony and distress that day.

Rose's Gift shop was a small white building with red and white window awnings overhanging the sidewalk. A sign reading "Rose's Gift Shop" hung down from its supporting frame, nearly touching the lawn and preventing mowing underneath. Unkempt grass grew around the posts and under the sign. This was definitely not Ralph's place. A side entrance led into the store, off the gravel alley.

Unlike Ralph, Rose did have a verbal greeting when I entered.

"Get out! I told your mother you're not to come in here. Don't touch anything!"

She was behind a counter at the opposite end of the shop, smoking a cigarette. Her hair was teased to conceal that it was thinning. Bright red lipstick and rouge stood out on her pale skin.

Figure 9 - Inside Rose's Gift shop

But her face flushed as she continued her verbal assault, frantically puffing on her cigarette.

"I'm going to call your mother! Your father! Get out! Don't touch anything!"

I had to deduce from Ralph's facial expressions that I wasn't welcome in his shop, but not so with Rose. However, I had a very different response. My devilish side made me linger.

The shop was crammed with display cases full of myriad knickknacks, figurines, goo-gahs, plates, bowls and the like—all made of glass. The cases had glass shelves and stood five feet high, with narrow aisles between them. I would walk quickly down an aisle, reach to the very back of a shelf, pick up the most fragile looking glass figurine and somehow maneuver it from the back of the crowded shelf. Holding it up to the light I pretended to examine its beauty, but really I was looking at Rose, who continued to frantically puff away.

"Put that back!" she cried, cigarette smoke billowing from her mouth. "I've told you not to come in here! I'm calling your mother!"

Alas, I enjoyed prolonging her agony. Then I reversed the figurine's journey to the back of the shelf.

Sometimes I enlisted my neighborhood friend Bill Davis to go in with me. We would go to opposite sides of the store so she couldn't see us both at the same time. Puffing on her cigarette, her head would sweep back and forth as she tried to keep track of us.

"You boys get out of here!" she bellowed. "I'm going to call both of your mothers!"

Later that summer, I noticed Ralph's grass was long and hadn't been cut. This was definitely unusual. I walked down the alley and his shop was closed. I didn't know what, but something wasn't right.

The next day I was raking leaves in my front yard and heard a loud "pop!" Shortly thereafter a police car arrived, followed by a hearse from Burns Funeral Home. I crossed the street and walked down the alley. Lying near the garage was something covered with a white sheet. I could see a trail of blood emerging from underneath. As I ventured closer, the Sheriff noticed me.

"Mike, stop! Don't come any closer."

"What happened?" I asked.

"Ralph killed himself," the Sheriff responded. "Suicide. Shot himself in the head."

I had heard of suicide, but to me it was just a word, a strange and frightening concept. Now it had happened to Ralph!

How could it be? I had seen him in his shop just a few days before, although we hadn't spoken. What would cause someone to do that to himself? Suddenly I realized that was Ralph's blood trickling from under the white sheet!

I later asked my parents about what I had seen. They said Ralph had been having a hard time since returning from the war. He had experienced a lot during his time in the Navy and wouldn't talk about it with anyone.

Months later I heard my parents talking about Rose being in the hospital. She came home, but never reopened her shop. A month later she died from lung cancer.

I'm sure I didn't harass Ralph enough to make him kill himself and I didn't give Rose lung cancer. I may have made Ralph want to smoke or Rose want to kill herself, but not the other way around.

***

I served in the U.S. Navy for seven years, after I had already become a physician. I did diving research for the U.S. Navy Experimental Diving Unit in Washington, D.C. I never saw combat or those injured in battle. However, what I did in the Navy was hazardous. Six of us were pressurized to the equivalent of 1,000 feet below sea level in an aboveground diving chamber for ten days. It was research to determine the effect of sea pressure on the human body. Two men were accidentally incinerated in a diving chamber fire two years before my arrival. Although dangers were involved, it was not combat. I received "hazardous duty pay" like our troops, but I wasn't being fired at.

What Ralph experienced during his Navy service is unknown, but it probably contributed to his suicide. It remains a huge problem with our troops, both during and after deployment. More than 6,500 military personnel commit suicide every year, more than the total number of soldiers killed in Afghanistan and Iraq combined since those wars began.

Judge McGill and Charlie

Judge Tom McGill and his brother Charlie lived next door to us with their sister Mary and her husband Raymond Davis. Tom was the County Judge, a tall, stately man with a serious personality. His brother Charlie, on the other hand, although tall, was awkward, heavy and tended to drool. He usually carried a handkerchief in his right hand to remedy the latter condition. Charlie worked for Raymond at Otasco Supply (Oklahoma Tire and Supply Company).

I'm not sure how Raymond felt about marrying Mary and inheriting her two brothers, but he spent a lot of time in his garage and shop, which was great for a kid looking for something to do. Raymond had a bottle "hid out" in his workshop, but I never knew him to over-indulge. Raymond would take Bill (his son), my brother and me camping on the nearby lakes.

Judge McGill loved golf. Every afternoon he was out in the yard practicing his swing and every weekend he played golf in the nearby town of Rogers. He would line up, set and swing at every leaf and twig in the front and side yard. One weekend he took his nephew Bill and me with him to Rogers for his golf outing. I remember it like it was yesterday because I was bored nearly to death. Slower golf has never been played before or since. I've always liked golf as a polite gentlemen's game, a time to relax and enjoy a walk with friends in beautiful places, but back then I surely thought I would die. Bill and I had to hold still and be quiet, two difficult tasks for small boys.

Finally, after the tee shots, we were off to the fairway. The Judge's beautiful swing was off that day and his second shot dribbled only a few yards, as did his third. He was frustrated, but had a solution. He calmly withdrew a tee from his pocket, teed the ball up in the fairway and whack…on the green, no problem. Thank all merciful heavens it was only a nine-hole course.

Charlie was…well, Charlie. There are several people in my past who we…well, harassed and Charlie was one. He stuttered and we knew that the more excited he got the more he stuttered. Bill Davis (Charlie's nephew) was kind of mean (my excuse). We would start asking Charlie questions and cuttin' up. He would try to answer us, but before he could we would ask another question…and on and on until Charlie couldn't speak for his stuttering.

Surely we deserve to burn in hell for what we did. If there is a big settling up in the sky, I may be in trouble on account of Charlie and Mr. Parker (our high school math teacher, who was the victim of a fake "electric shock" experiment).

Mr. and Mrs. Berry

Mr. and Mrs. Elliot Berry lived directly across West Central Avenue from us. They were an elderly retired couple. He was in the state legislature for a time, but now he was "taking it easy." Every evening after supper, weather permitting, they would sit out on their front porch. There were two elm trees in their front yard, one on each side of the short path leading to their front steps. The elm tree on the left was perfect for climbing, with a low branch for an initial ascent and several branches above where you could comfortably sit and be hidden from passers-by.

Mr. Berry smoked a pipe that required frequent lighting. Once it was dark you would see the flash of a match and his face glowing from the light, followed in a minute or two by the aroma of tobacco. The area in front of the porch was only sparsely covered with grass and collected the burnt matchsticks. I periodically harvested them as raw material for various projects, such as fence posts for the roads in my villages of sand.

One warm Saturday night in July when my cousin Billy was visiting from Fort Smith, we retrieved a clothes hanger and an old T-shirt from my closet. We hung the T-shirt on the hanger, splattered it with ketchup and climbed the elm in the Berry's yard. We tied a string to the coat hanger, positioned ourselves directly over the sidewalk and waited, ready to lower the "bloody" shirt onto unsuspecting passersby.

Figure 10 - Scaring passersby

Finally a couple came walking by. We lowered the shirt and jerked the string a few times. The couple screamed and ran off in apparent terror. Next an elderly woman walked by and again ran for her life. That was enough for one night.

Although she didn't tell me until years later, my mother had called our neighbors, the Jacksons and Mrs. Bryant and asked them to play their parts. It didn't matter. We still had fun.

Mr. Parker and Mr. Porter

I regret how I treated Mr. Parker, our high school math teacher. We cut up in his class so badly that I still feel guilty. He was quite elderly and hard of hearing. What made this worse was that he lived next door to us, upstairs in Mrs. Ida Tinnin's house. We threw spitballs at the blackboard and acted wild, but the worst episode in his class was the Model-T spark coil caper.

Some student brought a Model-T spark coil and battery into class in a briefcase. (I can't remember who, but I can find out because he was probably the only kid in Bentonville who had a briefcase back then). The spark coil was a transformer that converted six volts DC to high voltage AC to fire the spark plugs of a Ford Model-T. We had some fine wire that could hardly be seen, but when hooked up to the output side of the spark coil it could shock the piss out of you. This thing was a 1950s Taser gun.

Jim Tinnin, David Johnson, Keith Payne and I sat in armchair desks hooked together at the bottom by wooden runners. The briefcase person passed the wire and we were supposed to hook it to the four chairs in front of us. Instead, we connected the four of us. On the count of three we all started screaming, jumping and shaking. Then David fell on the floor in apparent agony. The wire wasn't even hooked up to the spark coil. Mr. Parker came back to see what was going on.

"Oh, Mr. Parker! Mr. Parker, look at this wire!"

He traced it back to the briefcase and the battery and spark coil were discovered. The poor innocent briefcase person was sent to the principal and we got off scot free. It's curious that I can't remember who he was…there has to be some reason why I can't remember.

Our history teacher, Mr. Porter, was another memorable teacher. First, Mr. Porter drove a Volkswagen when he came to Bentonville. I had never seen or heard of a foreign car, let alone a Volkswagen from Germany. The car was so small your knees pressed against the dashboard. Why would anyone want something so small? And an air-cooled engine? We were all just amazed.

Mr. Porter had clear ideas about how to maintain order in class. Looking back on it, I'm struck by the changes since those days. He believed in the "board" of education, a long wooden paddle with tapered handle. There were multiple holes in the business end, so air wouldn't impede its rapid movement toward the target area of those students who disturbed class in any way.

It was tough to be quiet and behave in Mr. Porter's class. He taught history…Arkansas history. Oh my, how boring. There were few students—boys, that is—who escaped the meetings with Mr. Porter after class. His classroom was off the backstage area of the auditorium. On the walls were the names of everyone who had been in a play or performance.

Figure 11 - Mr. Porter meting out punishment

David and I were requested to meet with Mr. Porter after class for talking or laughing or something. We knew this would be bad. He was delayed in class just long enough for us to slip newspapers down the back of our pants. He arrived, instructed us to bend over and whack!

We knew to scream with each of the licks and increased the volume as the punishment continued. Mr. Porter suspected something because I heard him muttering, but he wasn't sufficiently convinced of foul play to inspect our pants. It was a close one, but we had pulled it off! David and I were barely able to contain ourselves. Once outside, we laughed our heads off. We were supposed to get a lickin' and cheated the devil of his due. How sweet it was.

Chapter Three

Downtown

Nowhere But Everywhere To Go

I lived on West Central Avenue two blocks from downtown Bentonville. West Central Avenue was dubbed "Silk Stocking Row" supposedly because the women who lived there could afford silk stockings, a luxury at that time. Many of the homes on West Central were larger than most in Bentonville but there were numerous homes all over town larger and more elegant. The "Silk Stocking" label must have set West Central apart, however, I never saw myself as different.

Because of my proximity to downtown, I explored it often. One hot humid summer day after getting a glass of water at the soda fountain in Applegate's Rexall Drugstore I continued south, past the Cozy Theater, into the Bentonville Mercantile where Mr. Franklin warned, "Mike, don't touch anything! Your hands may be dirty."

Walton's 5 and 10 was next door and looked more interesting than the clothing store with its large glass windows and bright fluorescent lights. Upon entering, I walked quickly past the women's area where I could see bras and panties just lying there in plain sight! Then on to the toy area and my favorite, the hardware counter. After looking at the nuts, bolts and screws for a while, I continued to explore Sam's store.

At the back of the store, I saw unpainted rough wooden stairs leading to an elevated platform. From where I was, the platform looked small but I could see from up there I would have a view of the entire store. I wanted the view from above. On the platform was a man sitting at a desk completely consumed as he studied papers and made notes. He didn't notice me as I took the first step, but before I could take another, I felt a tap on my shoulder and the quiet stern voice of Bob Bogle, the store manager, "Mike, Sam's up there and he's real busy."

"Yes, Mr. Bogle I'll come back when Sam isn't so busy." Although I didn't know it at the time, I had left Sam to continue his creation of Wal-Mart.

Back out to the "eight-sided" square and my walk around town. There were many more stores to see, people with stories to tell and events to experience. I was only seven years old.

I had nowhere but everywhere to go. It was Bentonville, Arkansas in the 1950s.

Crow Drugstore and the Pharmacist

During the sticky, humid summer of 1955, I turned 11. "I Like Ike!" echoed from our Philco radio. Sunday school prayers were answered and "our boys" came home from Korea (even though I never knew where Korea was). Most people were working and Social Security protected the elderly. The Salk vaccine conquered polio and we returned to the swimming pool. These were naïve and simple times, as I was gliding through my youth in rural northwest Arkansas.

I had heard about television but had never seen one. They were in big cities, but this was a town of 3,000 nestled in the foothills of the Ozark Mountains. The closest "big cities" were Joplin, Springfield and Tulsa. Bentonville was less than twenty miles from Missouri and Oklahoma, but it could have been 1,000 miles because people had profound loyalties to their home states. "People in those other states are different," the old timers said, "not to be trusted." Bentonville was a quiet little town where people moved slowly, especially in the heat of August.

Located near the eight-sided "square" on West Central Avenue was the Crow Drugstore. Situated between Putnam's Ready-To-Wear and the Horseshoe Cafe, it had huge glass windows that covered the entire front of the store. It had a real old-time soda fountain with granite countertops and stools. Further back there were several black marble tables with padded chairs and four red booths. Ice cream sundaes, chocolate and vanilla milkshakes and malts, Coca-Cola and root beer floats. Crow Drugstore was my hangout.

They also had air-conditioning, the first and only store in town providing wonderful relief from the heat and sticky skin. But there was suspicious talk around town about this new luxury. Anything that felt so good had to be bad for the body, people said, although the exact nature of the damage was unknown.

That concern was far from my mind as I sat, cool and dry, watching Zelda create a sundae of vanilla ice cream, marshmallow topping, whipped cream and a maraschino cherry on top. Because she was the mother of a friend of mine, Zelda was always good for a little extra topping and whipped cream.

Pure pleasure for an 11 year old boy. Each spoonful required some change in technique to get the proper delightful combination of ice cream, marshmallow and whipped cream. I saved the maraschino cherry for the end, tilting the goblet to gather it in. I sat at the counter completely fulfilled, delightfully unaware of my surroundings until Mr. Caruthers , the pharmacist, passed in front of me in silence.

Mr. Caruthers was a big man, usually only seen in the pharmacy's elevated window. Shelves filled with bottles of pills covered the wall behind him. During the school year the soda fountain and tables were packed with noisy kids. Leaning forward in his window, he'd say, "Be quiet, I'm trying to hear the doctor."

The only other customer that day was Mr. Jackson, who was shopping at the other side of the store. Zelda cleared my empty goblet as Mr. Caruthers passed behind her without comment or greeting. I sat in silence as well, on the counter stool closest to the front of the store. The peanut-warming machine to my left displayed many kinds of nuts in a rotating carousel piled high to the edges, parading the choices for all who passed; except for peanuts and cashews, most were unknown to me. Daylight streamed in through the solid glass front door and illuminated the black-and-white tiled floor.

Mr. Caruthers leaned back against the counter. Smoking a cigarette and staring blankly toward the front of the store, he seemed content just looking at the light of day. With no warning he collapsed, colliding with the peanut machine, shaking nuts from the carousel. He landed on the tiled floor on his back, his head striking the floor with an unnerving "crack." He exhaled in a gush, his eyes open and unblinking, staring at the ceiling.

Zelda and I looked at each other. Mr. Jackson came over quickly, then slowed and stopped when he saw Mr. Caruthers' pale white face and empty eyes. Cautiously he felt his wrist, gently returned it to the floor and backed away. Not taking his eyes off the body, he said, "Zelda, call for a doctor." She finally got through to one, then picked up Mr. Caruthers' still smoldering cigarette from the floor.

A moment before I had been enjoying my marshmallow sundae, relishing the escape from the August humidity and Mr.

Caruthers had been standing ten feet away, enjoying his cigarette. He was still ten feet away, but now he was dead.

I had experienced death before when my neighbor Ralph shot himself, but this was different. Ralph had been covered with a white sheet. That was all I knew, my total experience with death. (My father would not pass away for a few more years, when I was 13.) There was no sheet covering Mr. Caruthers. I looked down at the face of death and shuddered.

I sat immobilized at the counter, overwhelmed and in shock. I tried to understand what I had just seen and heard. I needed to move this still conscious experience to some deeper part of my brain, where it could be isolated and suppressed, at least for now.

"Mike, I think you should go outside," Zelda suggested.

I agreed, with welcome relief. Standing up brought me closer to Mr. Caruther's body, which blocked my direct path to the front door. I backed up and circled around through the store and went outside. A half dozen people stood in the middle of the street in the full sun.

Figure 12 - Mr. Caruthers collapses to the floor

Why in the street? Was the sidewalk too close to the front door? They apparently hadn't seen me come out; they didn't know I had witnessed everything. They had only heard that Mr. Caruthers was "sick."

Sick? Mr. Caruthers was dead. I had seen him die.

Annie Graves came over from the Bentonville City Library, two doors down. She'd heard the news. A period of silence ensued and then Annie spoke with a resolute authority: "It was that air conditioning that killed him."

Killed by the air conditioning? I had heard the talk before, but now Mr. Caruthers was dead. Annie was the librarian, so she should know. We all stood staring at the glass front door of Crow Drugstore. Then someone spoke.

"Yes, it was the air conditioning." More silence. "God rest his soul. Amen. Amen."

Dr. Rollow arrived, carrying his black doctor bag and scurried inside. Five minutes passed and he emerged, head down, not looking at the crowd. His face reflected what I already knew.

A hearse arrived and double-parked. Bob Burns, the undertaker and an assistant removed the gurney and went inside. There was complete silence now. The crowd had backed up against the cars parked on the opposite side of the street, as far as possible from the hearse.

The gurney that reappeared now carried Mr. Caruthers feet first, covered with a blue blanket and secured by a brown leather strap. People scooted their feet back, attempting to get further away, as though they didn't want to catch anything. It seemed like no one took a breath until the hearse doors closed and carried Mr. Caruthers away.

Over the next few days my mother and I discussed what had happened and each conversation ended with the same questions. What happens when we die? Where is Mr. Caruthers now? Mother had no answers, nor did I.

For two weeks I didn't go near Crow Drugstore. When I walked past I remembered Mr. Caruthers' face and how it had happened so quickly. I could still see the face of death, but I was able to block it out and think of something else. My mind had built a wall around that memory so that it wasn't so overwhelming.

Living just a block from downtown, I went there often. People passing by Crow Drugstore would quicken their step and veer close to the curb, away from the front door. Something produced by the air conditioning might escape from the store and cause them to…well, whatever happened to Mr. Caruthers.

However, I was drawn back to the store, drawn to go inside. I was willing to risk death for a marshmallow sundae.

I stood halfway in the doorway, allowing my body to gradually adapt to the temperature change. Then I stood just inside the door, waiting for the first twinge of anything that didn't feel right, ready to run outside. Finally, I walked over to the soda fountain and sat down, monitoring my every breath and heartbeat.

Deep breath…nothing happened. I was still alive.

"Zelda, could I have a marshmallow sundae, please?"

Happily, it tasted the same as before Mr. Caruthers had died…delicious!

Crow Drugstore kept their air conditioner and over the next few years every business in town acquired one. The memory of Mr. Caruthers' death faded from everyone's memory—but not from mine.

I had seen him die. I had seen the face of death. He would not be my last.

Alvin Seamster and a Trip Back To the Civil War

Alvin Seamster was a Civil War buff. He had walked every inch of the Pea Ridge Battlefield in Arkansas. He either found or was given thousands of artifacts from the battlefield.

If you look on a map of the Civil War states, you find the Union in blue and the Confederate in gray. In the case of Northwest Arkansas and a few other areas, you'll find them in hatched black and white, meaning they never declared themselves for the North or South. The area of northwest Arkansas where I was born and raised was one of these hatched areas. This always confused me as a child, because I didn't know if we won or lost "The Waaar." An old-timer with whom I spoke didn't make it any better when he explained that we were on the side of whichever army was moving through town at the time. It made me feel like we were wimps without conviction.

Alvin had a second floor office on West Central in downtown Bentonville. He had three rooms, connected by doorways made through brick walls…brick made by and laid by my Irish Haneys in the 1880s and 1890s.

I'm not sure how I found my way to Alvin's office, but once I stepped through his open door I was transported back to the Civil War. He spent hours showing me the thousands of artifacts he loved and allowed me to experience the fear the soldiers felt during that incredible war.

The rooms were filled with muskets, musket balls, cannonballs, cooking utensils, canteens and everything else imaginable from the Pea Ridge battlefield. On one wall a rack contained 40 or 50 muskets of various vintages and types. Although the cap lock musket had largely replaced flintlock muskets during the Civil War, some flintlocks had been used.

Alvin explained how the flintlock musket mechanism delivered the spark to ignite the pan containing gunpowder, which then sent a flame into the barrel to fire the weapon. This sequence of events took one or two seconds, during which time the marksman had to aim steadily and ignore the flint striking the steel and the flash of gunpowder exploding in the pan before the weapon fired.

The 1950s were a time of southern domination of national politics by powerhouses like Fulbright, McClelland and Wilbur Mills, all from Arkansas. They passed legislation to repay the good people of Arkansas for sending them to Washington for forty years. One of these bills was the creation of the Pea Ridge National Battlefield in 1954.

To hear Alvin and others tell it, this was a decisive battle that turned the war for the North. Something about cutting off the supply lines to the south. For Alvin Seamster, the birth of the Pea Ridge National Battlefield permanently protected the place he loved. He donated numerous artifacts and they held a recognition ceremony for him. Alvin died shortly thereafter. He must have felt his life was full and complete, that the past went on living thanks to his efforts and enthusiasm. Thank you, Alvin, for taking a little kid back to the Civil War.

Charlie Cox: Simple Happiness

In 1950s Bentonville it was a point of pride that we had no stoplights and no parking meters. When they put a stoplight at West Central Avenue and A Street, people complained so much that they took it down. U.S. Highway 71 used to go through downtown and long-haul trucks would stop at this intersection, wind up through their gears and then head north to Missouri or south to the Boston Mountains. Later they built a Highway 71 bypass, but lying in bed on summer nights I could still hear the trucks through my windows, carried on the cool breeze along with the smell of freshly mown hay. The sounds and smells of youth linger forever.

With no suburbs, shopping centers, or malls, everything was in downtown Bentonville. There were no large parking lots and the locals always complained that street parking was limited. The solution was to limit downtown parking to two hours. Since parking meters were not an option, Charlie Cox was the solution, the right man for this job.

He walked the entire downtown every hour. He had a cut-off pool cue with chalk attached to the end by a battery clamp.

The streets with two-hour parking were limited to the immediate downtown area: diagonal parking around the city square and parallel parking on West Central Avenue, North Main Street, South Main Street, East Second Street and West Second Street. Charlie took a one and a half mile walk through the town, marking the left rear tire of every car with chalk.

That amounted to about 80 cars every hour and he issued a parking ticket to any car with three chalk marks (meaning that it had been parked for more than two hours). Charlie would always stop and chat, but only for a few minutes, then excuse himself by saying, "I have to continue my rounds."

Charlie made eight rounds a day of a mile and a half each, so that's 12 miles a day and marking 80 cars every hour meant over 600 chalk marks a day.

Yes, a few people would wipe the chalk off, but not many. It was easier to move the car and not cheat. Besides, the ticket wasn't very much.

Barbershop Memories

When I was three years old, my mother took me to Harley's Barber Shop (previously the Elkhorn) for my first haircut. Harley put a white wooden board across the arms of the chair, the paint worn through in the center from all the wiggly kids. Mother stood nearby coaxing me to hold still. Back then behavior was important to a family's reputation; my mother's presence assured her boys would behave.

Almost everything is new to a little kid and Harley's Barber Shop was no exception. Several people sat in wooden chairs opposite the row of four barber chairs. There were mirrors behind the barbers and on the opposite wall above the chairs. The reflection of their reflections took a few head turns to figure out. Everyone was talking and laughing. Every new laugh required an additional turn of the head to see what was going on.

As I got older Mother didn't have to go with me. She would give me the money and I went alone. Holding still was easier, once you had most of the sounds figured out. I remember one such visit on a windy, cool autumn day. It was Saturday, so the farmers were in town. I was around eight years old. Upon entering Harley's there was a hat and coat rack to the left of the door. Toward the back a wooden cabinet with glass windows contained piles of bandages and tape. I was curious why they had bandages in a barbershop. I sat down to wait for my turn. Harley was cutting a farmer's thinning hair. From a child's point of view, it seemed a waste of time to cut the little hair the man had left.

"Mr. Harley, why do you have those bandages?"

"Mike, years ago barbers performed some of the services that doctors do today."

"Why do you still have them?" I continued.

"You never know what could happen in here. One of these guys could slip and cut someone's ear off and we would need them. Come on, Mike, you're next."

Several of the local men went in every morning for their shaves. The barbers would wrap their faces with a steaming hot towel, then work up the lather in their personal mugs (kept in a white cabinet at the back of the shop). Most mugs were white, but they also had designs in every color and shape imaginable. My dad's mug was in the third row down, second from the left, embossed with "JOE" in gold letters.

After applying the lather, the barber would strop the straight razor on the leather and begin the shave. After each stroke of the razor, the barber would wipe the lather on the back of his free hand. The barber and his customer could be having a lively discussion, but when the razor went to the face all talk suddenly ceased. As soon as he finished one cheek, talk resumed exactly where they left off. When the barber rounded the chair to shave the opposite cheek, conversation once again halted. It was like the high school band director when he raised his baton—everyone stopped talking and readied their instruments.

How relaxing it must have been to start your day lying back in a barber's chair, your face warm from hot towels, ready to be soaped up and shaved.

Harleys closed in the late 50s when I was 12 years old. The invention of the safety razor made it quick and easy for men to shave themselves at home. Barbershops were once a necessity, but within a few years they became a luxury. Why pay someone to do something you could do yourself?

My dad knew a good thing. He got the last shave at Harley's before they closed the shop.

***

Harley's was replaced by the Mayhall Barbershop. While Harley's was old fashioned, the new barbershop was modern looking; it had metal chairs with plastic cushions.

The Mayhall brothers opened the shop when they returned from the Korean War. They learned to cut hair when they served in the U.S. Army. Army haircuts are rather basic and, luckily for them, the basic burr haircut was in style when they returned. Then after a few years the flat top came into style and they mastered that cut. After the flat top came Elvis, the ducktail and Brylcreem. The Mayhall Brothers were put to the test and the ducktail was their downfall. When I was a teenager I remember going in and getting a haircut from Johnny Mayhall.

"Leave the sides long," I told him, "but take a little off the top, please."

When he finished I had a burr on top and a ducktail on the sides. I took one look in the mirror and told Johnny, "That is the worst haircut I've ever had."

He just shook his head. "I'll try to do better in two weeks. Next!"

Attorney Charles Gocio: Revenge in Advance

I got in first licks on Mr. Charles Gocio, attorney-at-law, when I was young and innocent. He may have wanted to prosecute me and send me to jail, but he couldn't...and here's why.

Jimmy Tinnin had gotten a new machete for Christmas and we went out looking for something to cut. We took off behind Jimmy's house and came upon a vacant lot filled with tall grass and a few small saplings. We made quick work of the saplings and continued on our quest to fight the Koreans or some other foe.

A week or so later my folks told me Attorney Gocio had contacted them and Jimmy's parents. He was planning to build a new house on the lot in a few years and had planted the saplings so that he might have trees someday.

Whoops! How were we to know? I'm sure he was frustrated as hell, but there was nothing he could do.

Belle Starr

I collected coins and stamps during my pre-teen years. I would take a few dollars and all my change to the Bank of Bentonville and exchange them for coins I hopefully didn't have. I would take them home, search through them and be back to the bank the same day. I repeated this scenario several times a week and the tellers rarely batted an eye. In fact, one day Audrey Robbins took me downstairs to the vault. We walked in through a huge gray metallic door and the walls were lined with steel drawers and shelves storing papers and files. To the left of the door was a safe five feet high. Audrey opened it to reveal stacks of cash. It seemed like all the money in the world. I asked which money belonged to my family and Audrey pointed to a stack at the back.

On another day, a teller named Josephine asked me if I knew about Belle Starr robbing and shooting up the bank. I responded that I didn't. She explained that in the 1920s Belle Starr and her gang came into the bank and announced a stickup. A nearly deaf elderly man had his back to her and kept on talking to one of the bank officials. To get his attention, Belle fired her gun. The poor man heard the discharge, turned to see Belle with a six-shooter and collapsed into a nearby chair. She collected what cash there was and made her getaway into Missouri, only to be caught a few months later. Josephine pointed to a hole high on the window jamb where a bullet was still lodged.

I had a friend read the draft of this story and, unfortunately, very little of the Belle Starr story is correct. Belle Starr had a colorful criminal past, but she died in 1889, killed when she was shot in the back by one of four people. The suspects included an outlaw with whom she had been feuding, a former lover, her husband and her son; the actual killer was never identified. Wow! Belle told *The Fort Smith Elevator*: "I regard myself as a woman who has seen much of life."

Indeed, it was Henry Starr who robbed the "People's Bank of Bentonville" in 1893. Henry was Belle's nephew by marriage and he robbed more banks than all of the better known gangs combined. Henry met his demise years later when he robbed the bank in Harrison, Arkansas and was shot by the former bank president.

There were several bandits who robbed banks in Arkansas and surrounding states. The reason was that prior to 1907 Oklahoma wasn't a state. It was the Indian Territory and this provided some legal protection from extradition. Bentonville was only 18 miles west of Oklahoma and the first city of any size.

The Doctors

There were three physicians in Bentonville during my time: Dr. Rollow, Dr. Compton and Dr. Jackson. Dr. Rollow was our family doctor and treated my father. Dad smoked three packs of Camels a day, had severe high blood pressure (the Army wouldn't take him) and always ate bacon and eggs for breakfast and steaks for dinner. He went on drinking binges for one to two weeks at a time, during which he smoked more. I'm sure Dad wasn't Dr. Rollow's best patient. After Dad's first heart attack in 1957, he continued to have chest pain, developed fluid on his lungs and couldn't breathe. Dr. Rollow did all he could. He would come by the house day or night to do an EKG and gave Dad shots of morphine and diuretics. These helped for a time. Dr. Rollow was a prime example of a first-rate family doctor.

Dr. Compton was an interesting man of depth. He practiced general medicine, but his love was nature. He was still living in the Compton home on North Main during my youth. He was solely responsible for saving the Buffalo River in Northern Arkansas from being dammed and was responsible for the creation of the Buffalo River National Park.

Dr. Compton was one of the few men who was comfortable showing and expressing his feminine side, which I found interesting. My stepfather Gordon Knott was another. Gordon grew orchids, while Dr. Compton loved all kinds of flowers. He had forty acres that adjoined our forty-acre "Slaughter Pen Hollow." Dr. Compton's land was planted with exotic plants and flowers and our land was used to slaughter pigs and graze cattle. His land was severely infested with kudzu plants and ours wasn't. I think the cows on our land ate the young kudzu plants.

Jim Walton hired high school kids to cut the kudzu off the former Compton property, but the kudzu grew faster than they could chop. It was a losing battle, but it kept the high school kids off the streets.

Dr. Jackson lived in the red brick Haney-Knott house on South Main and practiced general medicine. I guess he was bored, because he took classes on hypnotism at the University Of Arkansas School Of Medicine in Little Rock.

I went to see him to have a cyst removed from my left cheek. My brother was with me. I told Dr. Jackson I was worried about the shots hurting. He suggested that he hypnotize me so it wouldn't hurt. He demonstrated it on my brother. He told Joe to relax and close his eyes, and then pinched the skin of Joe's arm with a medical clamp. It looked like it didn't hurt, at least as far as I could tell. (Joe told me later it did hurt, but he didn't want to say anything at the time.)

I was convinced by the demonstration, so Dr. Jackson hypnotized me, told me the shots wouldn't hurt and they didn't. He made the incision, removed the cyst and sewed me up, no problem. I was now a believer in hypnosis. Joe and I tried it on each other, but it didn't work. Must have needed the doctor's clout.

I wished Zella, Dr. Jackson's nurse, used hypnotism. Every spring I had terrible hay fever as a kid. Mother took me to the Oklahoma Allergy Clinic for skin testing and they prescribed twice a week shots. Once when Zella thrust the needle in me, I thought I would die. Tears welled up in my eyes. She made some remark about the needle needing sharpening and when she withdrew it I almost passed out. She held it up, wiped it with a cotton ball and the needle snagged the cotton, revealing that the tip was bent. Let's hear it for disposable needles.

Chapter Four

Growing Up

Walnut Business

When I was eight years old, I heard a company in Hiwasse, Arkansas would pay $6 for a hundred pounds of walnuts in the husk or $10 per hundred pounds out of the husk. I didn't think twice—I wanted the double-digit money to buy a new bike. The 20" Schwinn Racer was only six bags of husked walnuts.

Our next-door neighbor, Mrs. Ida Tinnin, had two large walnut trees in her backyard and walnuts covered the ground. I asked her if I could have them and she agreed. All I had to do was remove the husks and get them to Hiwasee. Dad said he would drive the walnuts and me the 18 miles when I had them ready. Everything was arranged and I was nearly riding my bike.

I raked up a big pile of green walnuts and sat down on an overturned bucket with my pocketknife. I was carving away, only to discover that the husks remained firmly attached. I had worked for two hours and only had thirty or so walnuts ready for market. I needed a mechanized approach.

Figure 13 - Husking walnuts

I noticed that the walnuts in our rear driveway split open when cars ran over them. The driveway was two hundred feet long and had ruts. I gathered all the walnuts from Mrs. Tinnin's yard and laid them in the ruts one layer deep. All I needed was Mom and Dad to drive over the beds a few times and the Schwinn Racer was mine.

I requested they use the rear driveway exclusively when going and coming. They agreed. After a week or so I had a flat bed of walnuts, but none were split open. I was even riding my old bike over them, with no effect. I asked my parents to make extra trips, yet it still wasn't working. At this point my enthusiasm was waning and I forgot the walnuts for a few weeks.

When I checked them again, the cars had done their work. The walnuts in the center of the ruts were beginning to split open. I also noticed they were turning black. I asked my parents to drive on the edges of the ruts to complete the job. They complied. In my dreams I was riding my new Schwinn bike.

At last most of the walnuts were split open and ready for harvest. However, I noticed that the husks had turned completely black and softened. It appeared the sun had ripened the husks, which made them rather sticky and gooey. Nevertheless, it was time for harvest. I bought eight gunnysacks from the Coop Feed Store for 5¢ each, which was my only cash outlay to date. I grabbed my bucket and began.

After two hours of enthusiastic work I had filled only half a bag. My face was black, my clothes were black, the walnut goo matted my hair and my hands were so sticky I could hardly open them.

Mercifully, Mother came out to check on my progress. She smiled and chuckled a bit as she cleaned me up with kerosene. After my face was again visible, I undressed on the back porch and was off to a hot bath with lots of soap.

Over the next few months the walnuts dried into a hard mat. Santa took mercy on me and I got the Schwinn Racer for Christmas.

Paul Brewer

Paul Brewer was nice to me, but his neighbors disliked him. He was a ham radio operator and the roof of his house and backyard looked like a military base, crammed into a one-quarter acre lot. In addition, when he was transmitting and keyed the mike, he blew out his neighbors' speakers, nearly making everyone deaf. The only people he didn't bother were in the cemetery about 100 yards west of his house.

Paul was a good man and the local shoe repairman. Brewer's Shoe Shop was on South Main. He had numerous grinders, buffers and brushes connected by a leather belt to a large motor. When you entered his shop, the glues, dyes, stains, waxes and polishes gave off wonderful odors, accented by a touch of burnt rubber.

Paul helped my friend Jimmy Plumlee and me get our novice ham radio licenses so we could transmit Morse code all around the world—well, at least to Minnesota. My call letters were KN5WSO, which I took to mean "World's Sharpest Operator." This should have been "World's Slowest Operator."

Well, I remember Paul Brewer talking about doing something different with his life. I don't know whether he smelled too many solvents, but he made a change and went to work for the Bentonville Police Department as a night patrolman.

While I missed the smells of his shop, his new job had huge benefits for me, at least in the beginning. Bentonville was in a "dry county" (still is), which meant that people had to go to Springdale, Tonitown, or to the "line" (Missouri state line) to get booze or go to a bar. Most people in town went to bed after the nine o'clock news on the Joplin station, but some people wanted more excitement. The really drunk ones would usually pass out in the bar or crash their cars before they got back to Bentonville, which made less work for Paul on the night shift.

I know this because starting about 3 a.m. he would let Jimmy Plumlee and me ride around with him in his patrol car. I would get up, get dressed and walk downtown to wait for him at Davidson's DX Gas Station.

The first couple of times he warned us in a very stern voice: "If there's an emergency on my shift, I'm going to put you out on the street wherever we are and you'll have to find your way home." That was very exciting to us, but of course it never happened. It was fun to be in a police car at night. Little did I know how that would change.

As I got older, I gravitated toward more mischievous activities. One summer an out-of-town kid was visiting his grandparents on Highway 71 toward Rainbow Curve. I was 15 at the time. He was two years older and wilder than me, my excuse for what was to follow.

One hot night we quietly pushed his grandparents' car out of their yard and went for a ride. After a while we stopped for apple pie a la mode at Zelda's Cafe. Shortly thereafter Paul came in with a serious look, walked slowly over to our table and arrested us for stealing the car. Oh my! He took us to the jail (not in handcuffs, thankfully, or I would have died).

During the drive, the rear seat of the police car had a different feel from riding around with Paul in the early morning hours. I was in tears. Mother came to the station, the charges were dropped shortly thereafter and I went home and directly to bed. I like to think it was the older kid's fault and it turned out he had a record in whatever town he came from. I never saw him again and that was fine with me.

I didn't see much of Paul Brewer after that incident. He was eventually elected police chief and didn't work nights. My novice ham radio operator's license had expired, I couldn't translate Morse code fast enough to get my general license and I had had enough of police cars.

Cleveland Boatman and the Great Pinball Caper

Perhaps Cleveland Boatman ended up in Silicon Valley at the head of some high-tech firm, but he started off in Bentonville. He always won the local, regional and state science fairs with some kind of electronic gadget. He once constructed a light board with electrical timers, relays and switches to show the movement of the planets. I remember Pluto never moved.

Cleveland helped me with my science fair projects. He was several years older than me and much smarter. We made the projects out of old pinball machine parts that Mr. Charles Marple sold us for $5.00 per machine (a real deal). Mr. Marple had the pinball and jukebox businesses for northwest Arkansas and southwest Missouri.

Cleveland knew a lot about pinball machines and we played the one at the Greyhound Bus station in downtown Bentonville. Like most kids, we always wanted to make enough points to win extra games. The machine was in the station waiting area, adjacent to the café. Most times the terminal was empty except for the ticket agent, who usually hung out in the café.

Cleveland had the idea that if we interrupted the electric power to the machine when the pinball fell into a scoring slot, we could prevent the kicker arm from ejecting the ball and score points until hell froze over. At least, that was the theory.

Figure 14 - Our switch connected to the pinball machine

I made a small box with a spring-loaded switch connected to a button on the outside. We could plug the pinball machine into the box and the box into the wall. By pressing the button with our feet we could interrupt the power and, hopefully, score big.

It was scary when we connected the box and started playing. It worked like a charm—every time we pressed it, the scoring wheel advanced until we had 20 game credits. I was trembling with excitement that we would be caught and...

And what? Thrown in jail for cheating a pinball machine?

There's a difference between stealing, murdering and cheating a pinball machine, but at that moment I would have been hard pressed to comprehend the difference. Cheating was thrilling, new and exciting. We played for hours, free.

Looking back, we were nothing but low-tech computer hackers. We weren't trying to make money, but neither are computer hackers today. Like them, we just wanted to see if we could do it. Times and kids don't change—just the machines they play with! Who knows? Cleveland Boatman's company is probably a computer security firm...what goes around, comes around. And it all started in the Greyhound Bus Terminal in Bentonville, Arkansas.

Briartowners vs. the Ivy League Boxer

Growing up in the 1950s in rural Arkansas wasn't easy for a shy, non-aggressive teen. Some kids were bullies and some just liked to fight. I was neither of these. To me, fighting was just scary.

My friend Lonnie (not his real name) liked to fight, but he wasn't a bully. He wasn't tall, but had massive shoulders and arms. As Saturday night approached he would start looking for an opponent. Luckily, I wasn't on his list of contenders. When Saturday arrived, Lonnie would have a fight set up with someone by mutual agreement and sometimes there was more than one taker.

One Saturday night the fight was held on the town square, across from the Benton County Courthouse and in front of Walton's Five and Ten. The event attracted 40 or 50 people, who provided a moving "ring" for the best show in town. The Bentonville police watched from their police car. It was as though they sanctioned the event, which seemed strange to me at the time. However, there were no knives or guns, just fists and I guess the cops appreciated that.

Before the fight began, Lonnie drank whiskey straight from the bottle, wiped his mouth with the back of his hand and let out a sigh. No Coca-Cola or ice to soften the sting—it was the effect he sought, not the taste.

Figure 15 - Saturday night fights on the town square

Then the main event was on. The fighting was wild, even occasionally bloody, with arms swinging everywhere and even some kicking. It never lasted long, maybe five minutes, ten tops. Lonnie always won.

I hated the violence. What had he really won? People would hold his bottle of whiskey until he was ready for another pull, hoping to placate Lonnie so he wouldn't focus on them for his next contender.

He was impressive to see after a fight—sweating, nose flaring with every breath, shoulders and arms held high, eyes wide, actively scanning those around him, looking for another challenger.

"Lonnie, here's your bottle."

When you don't like to fight, everyone knows it. You get picked on, not by the likes of Lonnie, but by every lightweight dumb-shit who wants to fight. I got picked on and was made to feel inferior and ashamed. It was a difficult part of growing up in the 1950s. There were times when I went home crying after someone tried to pick a fight with me. Twice I made a showing, but I just didn't have a violent nature. I always lost, but, in truth, I didn't even try.

One night about eight of us kids were hanging out at Zesto's, our local ice cream and hamburger joint. It was summertime and the air was filled with the smell of grilled hamburgers and new mown hay. It had been a hot August day and we were still sticky with sweat as the day cooled down and the breeze shifted.

I usually knew everyone hanging out at Zesto's, but that night there was an older kid I didn't know. He was quiet and dressed nicer than we local boys. He told us he wasn't originally from Bentonville, but that his parents had recently retired here. He attended college back East and was on summer break. He said he was flying back the next day.

As we were talking, a rusted car missing a front bumper drove up. It parked along the street, blocking the entrance to Zesto's. The driver got out, slammed the door and walked around the front of the car. He and his passenger were from Briartown, an area of Bentonville where the poorer families lived. Rough dirt roads, tarpaper shacks, parents and kids with rotten teeth.

"Any of you want a piece of my ass?" the driver snarled. He had obviously been drinking.

I knew these two guys and they were mean. One of them started pushing me around. *Here we go again,* I thought. The college kid watched him in silence, then walked up and said calmly, "Leave him alone, he's not bothering you."

Oh, Lord! He was from out of town, didn't know these Briartowners and was about to get his ass beat. Neither backed down and the lines were drawn.

One of the Briartowners shouted several four-letter words and lunged forward with his first swing. But before he could make any contact, the college kid assumed a strange, formal boxing stance, fists in front of his face and bouncing around on his toes. The Briartowner's first punch was easily deflected and then *whap, whap!* As quick as lightning, the college kid landed two blows to his opponent's face, knocking him back, stunned.

The Briartowner screamed several more insulting names and came back swinging.

Whap, whap!

Two more punches landed on the Briartowner's face. The college kid hadn't been touched. Blood streamed from the Briartowner's nose and a cut above his left eye. Unperturbed, he charged forward a third time.

Whap! Whap! Whap!

The Briartowner was knocked to the ground. He staggered to his feet, hand pressed to his damaged eye. He'd had enough.

My God in heaven, it was wonderful—victory for every "I don't like to fight kid" in the whole world, but mainly me.

But it wasn't over. The Briartowner's buddy shouted, "I'll show you how to fight, you…"

The college kid started bouncing again as his second opponent approached.

Whap! Whap! Whap! Nose, eye, cheek. And one more charge. CRUNCH!!! The sound made me shudder. The Briartowner's nose was broken. He staggered to their car, holding his face. Blood gushed from his nose and his left eye was nearly closed. He paused briefly, trying to find the car door handle and said, without conviction, "We'll be back."

I felt the humiliation and embarrassment of my past disappear. I bought the Ivy Leaguer a Coca-Cola. We talked as he drank his soda. Turned out he was a college boxer and his team had won the East Coast collegiate championship the previous year.

The West Central to Second Street Raceway

I was 11 years old when I told my father, "Dad, I want to get an old car. I want to remove the engine, take it apart and put it back together." I had no idea if he would get me one. Kids ask their parents for so many things that just pop into their heads.

The 1950s was one of those special times for American cars. Each year, every car company introduced a completely redesigned car with an entirely new look. In hindsight, the car companies spent all their profits on new designs. That's what America wanted and that's what the country got.

Teenage boys anxiously awaited the new car deliveries. They were unloaded in secrecy and covered with a cotton sheet in the showroom. I would quietly enter Burger Chevrolet through the side door, sneak over behind the hidden secret and unveil the rear bumper and fender.

Carl Burger surprised me from behind.

"Mike, two more days. No peeking."

"Just a quick look at the rear taillight?" I pleaded.

"Two more days."

Where did he come from, I wondered. But it wasn't surprising to have a salesman be that attentive. Today a whole herd of them will notice you turn into their lot, the year, make and model of your car, whether your tires are bald, etc., etc. Car salesmen were and are a special group.

It turned out that Mr. Alexander of Alexander's Used Cars owed Dad some money for his insurance policy premium and soon thereafter a dirty orange 1946 Studebaker appeared in our driveway completely unannounced. It would barely start and idled with a rhythmic, loping sound. After bloodying a few knuckles, I managed to change the oil, oil filter and spark plugs. Now the car started and ran like new.

Dad thought I had performed a miracle. He got all excited and said we could buy old cars, have me tune them up and resell them for a good profit. I kept telling him that all I did was change the spark plugs. I just got lucky and happened to fix the one wrong thing. I knew nothing about carburetors, electrical timing, generators, etc. I was a spark plug specialist and nothing more. Slowly Dad gave up his vision of big money and I was left with the Studebaker. I was barely 11 years old and couldn't see over the steering wheel.

In 1950s' Arkansas teens started driving when they were 13 ½. We couldn't get a driver's license until we were 16, but this legal requirement was overlooked because everyone knew the farm kids had to drive tractors and trucks to "get the crops to market." I'm not sure which crops they were talking about, because you couldn't grow much in the ground in northwest Arkansas, only chickens in houses. I guess they were picking up feed for the chickens or salt licks for the cattle.

Although we weren't farm kids we reaped the benefits and routinely drove at 13 ½ years old. Why 13 ½ and not 13 or 14, I do not know, but those were the "rules."

I got a speeding ticket when I was 15 and nervously went to the Bentonville city traffic court, as the ticket required. Judge Tom McGill, my neighbor, fined me $13 and there was no mention of the fact I didn't have a driver's license.

"Yes sir. Yes, your Honor." I paid cash and was out the door. That was the end of it. Whew!

I'm getting ahead of myself. Back to the '46 Studebaker. Eleven was too young to drive, even in Bentonville. Therefore, I had this car and couldn't drive on the streets. However, our driveway ran from West Central Ave. in front of our house to Second Street at the rear of our property. It was a straight shot, one block long, about 1/16th of a mile.

Well, not quite a straight shot, as there were three obstacles. First, the driveway went under our carport. Second, immediately after the carport there was a large tree on the right of the driveway. The driveway made a slight jog to the left around the tree and then curved back to the right to pass through the third obstacle, our garage. Yes, the driveway went through our garage. We had front and rear garage doors. Dad had the rear door added so he could drive out the back driveway if Mother's car was blocking his exit to the front. This was quite handy for Dad, but more important for me it doubled the length of our driveway.

I put the front seat of the Studebaker all the way forward, sat up straight and was off on my first run. Initially, I simply drove from West Central in front, under the carport, made a slight jog around the tree, through the garage and down the back driveway to Second Street. This was easy and exciting. I was driving!

Next, for an extra challenge, I added a little speed, since the garage was only a foot or so wider than the Studebaker. Still, no problem. I mastered this after a few runs. I added more and more speed. Eventually I would peel out in the front driveway, zoom under the carport at 10 m.p.h., around the tree at 15 m.p.h., through the garage at 20 m.p.h., head down the rear straightaway at a top speed of 30-35 m.p.h. and brake to a stop in a cloud of dust with the nose of the car protruding only slightly into Second Street, clutch smoking, gravel flying and engine steaming hot. I was King of the Bentonville 1/16th of a Mile Raceway. Wow! Definitely thrilling!

There was a row of tall shrubs at the back of our property, so no one could see me heading toward Second Street; this was not the case for West Central Ave., as we shall see.

After several runs, this route bored me. I had no one to compete with, so I had to devise a greater challenge.

I changed directions and drove from Second Street to West Central. This wasn't a problem for me, but was definitely one for the passing motorists on West Central. These innocent, unsuspecting motorists would be driving along, minding their own business and suddenly an orange blur would shoot out from beside our house, heading for them on a collision course. Several of them would panic and lock up their brakes to avoid an impending collision, only to watch me slide to a stop in a cloud of dust. There were numerous tire marks on both sides of West Central, left behind by some really pissed-off people.

Sometimes a car behind the braking one would nearly rear-end the one in front. Both drivers would honk their horns, shake their fists and yell at me, but to no avail. I was off on my next challenge—a southbound run to Second Street…in reverse

This took several days to master, but I gradually increased speed. I never went as fast in reverse, but I could go through the garage at 15-20 m.p.h. I didn't know the exact speed because speedometers don't work in reverse and, of course, I was looking behind me, trying to negotiate the garage. I was young, had good reflexes and learned quickly.

Next was traveling in reverse from Second Street to West Central. I'd emerge from the obstacle course of garage, tree and carport to once again slide to a stop just short of more terrified motorists on West Central. Their relief at having avoided a collision quickly turned to anger.

Figure 16 - Racing to West Central

"What do you think are you doing?"

Unfortunately, I couldn't hear them above the screech of my spinning tires and roaring engine as I was off on another run.

The West Central to Second Street Reverse Direction Run proved to be more challenging. I had to avoid the tree by correcting to the left, and then turn right in time to enter the garage in a straight manner. This was tricky. One time, after successfully passing the tree in reverse, I over-corrected, bringing the side fender into contact with the garage door hinge mechanism. It slammed shut just as I slid to a stop at Second Street. Talk about dramatic! It smacked of *special effects*! I could still hear the slamming door echoing around the neighborhood as the dust settled. I escaped with only a short scratch on the fender. Wow!

Still, I began to wonder if I should tone this down a little.

Alas, it was to be my final run. Mother had been observing my speedway performance and could take no more. She saw where this was going.

Her intervention came just in time, for I was planning the *Reverse Top Speed Rearview Mirror Only* event!

Cheap Perfume

I was involved in a few mischievous pranks in my life, but usually had one or more friends with me to share the creativity or blame. But there was one prank that I created and carried out all by myself.

It was a hot summer afternoon. I had just finished a marshmallow sundae at Crow Drug Store and was taking the back way home, walking down the alley between Putman's Ready-To-Wear and Bentonville City Hall. A Bell Telephone Company truck was parked at the end of the alley and a temporary work fence guarded an open manhole. Between the fence and the truck was a small fan with a yellow and black hose extending from it into the open manhole. I studied this device as I walked by, as I had never seen one before.

The fan's electric motor was hooked up to the truck for power and was apparently blowing fresh air to the worker below. I peered into the manhole and could see the top of a yellow hardhat. The worker was splicing together two telephone cables, each of which looked like it had two hundred wires. He didn't hear me above the blowing hum of the fan. Continuing toward home, I made a left and was halfway to Burger Chevrolet when the idea hit me.

Figure 17 - My devilish center contemplating a prank

I don't know where it came from; perhaps from a "devilish center" in my brain that periodically sent out mischievous messages: "Michael, what if you soaked a rag with some cheap perfume and put it in the air intake of that telephone man's fan?"

"What!" I exclaimed.

"You could get a little bottle of perfume at the Walton's Five and Ten," the voice went on. "You saw it there last week for only thirty five cents."

"What!" I said again.

"It wouldn't do him any harm, but he'd be very surprised and make a fast exit. You could watch from behind the cars and he'd never see you."

"Okay."

I was off to Walton's Five and Ten, bought the perfume, found an old rag behind the hardware store and was ready. I suddenly became terrified. I felt my heart pounding, my hands trembling.

"Why am I doing this?"

"Go ahead" came the command from the devilish center.

I was so afraid I'd get caught, but I soaked the rag, snuck up to the fan, put the rag just below the intake and ran like hell to the last car at Burger Chevrolet. My hands were visibly shaking.

I heard a shout: "What in the hell is going on here!" He was still in the manhole and I was half a block away and could still hear him.

Oh my, I thought.

Then I saw the yellow hard hat emerge from the manhole. He was a huge man with a full beard and big eyes scanning the area and he wasn't smiling.

"I'm going to get someone for this!"

Figure 18 – Running from the scene of the crime

I shuddered. I was afraid to run for fear he would see me between the cars. He picked up the rag, waved it by his nose and threw it down in disgust. He began to pace in larger and larger circles. Finally he disappeared into the alley and I had my chance.

I took off behind Burger Chevrolet and ran past the service department. Carl Burger was leaving and saw my panicked pace.

"Where's the fire?" he asked.

"Hello, Mr. Burger. I gotta get home. I...I...I heard my mother calling me." It was all I could think to say. I doubt he believed me, since I only lived 1½ blocks away.

I ran through the back door, into my room, lay down on my bed and told my devilish center: "Don't ever do that again."

Jimmy Pickens and the Hot Car

Dr. Pickens was a family friend and an eye, ear, nose and throat specialist. He worked and lived in the nearby town of Rogers, seven miles away. He and his wife Evelyn had two children, Jamie and Jimmy. Jamie was cute and bright. Jimmy, although pleasant, was like the rest of us boys…mischievous. During the age of the hormone storm, from 14 to 16 years old, we boys are full of power, curiosity and self-destruction, but totally lack common sense and judgment.

Dr. Pickens was successful and on a lark bought a new 1958 red Chevrolet convertible. Jimmy loved that car but was too young to drive at 14. To make things worse, Dr. Pickens seldom drove the car, saying, "It's too hot in the summer and too cold in the winter." This was in the days before good car air conditioners and Arkansas winters can be in the teens for several days running. It was torture for Jimmy to see the car just sit there and not be driven.

One day Dr. Pickens and Evelyn went fishing in War Eagle on White River. Jimmy knew they would be gone the entire day. He was home alone with only the convertible to keep him company. He knew where the extra keys were kept and couldn't resist the temptation any longer.

He was off on a fast drive on the back roads between Bentonville and Rogers. He laid rubber on Highway 12 toward Cave Springs, rounded Rainbow Curve at 70 m.p.h. and topped out at 95 m.p.h. on Highway 71 coming into Rogers, made a left into his driveway and parked the car in the carport.

Suddenly he was afraid his parents would discover he took the car without their permission and began to panic. What if they came home and noticed the engine was hot? He hooked up the garden hose, ran it to the carport, opened the hood and proceeded to hose down the engine. It made some grunting sounds and one metallic crack, but now it was cool. Jimmy returned the hose and retreated to the house. He was excited. What fun! He had pulled it off and all was well.

Not quite.

Dr. and Mrs. Pickens returned in late afternoon and the first thing they noticed was water under the Chevrolet. Further inspection revealed a mixture of green antifreeze and oil in the water. They quickly figured it out and Jimmy was caught.

It wouldn't have been so bad if the engine block wasn't cracked. Dr. Pickens sold the car for what he could get.

The sad part was that he was planning to give the car to Jimmy when he turned 15.

Bill Black and the Eagle Mill Racer

For several years in the mid-1950s stock car racing was popular in Bentonville. The engine had to be stock, but the rest of the car could be modified. They raced around an oval dirt track west of the local airport. Employees from the Eagle Milling Company (my stepfather's feed business) modified an old Ford and created the "Eagle Racer." But interest in racing faded and the car was retired, parked to rust in the rain.

My friend Bill Black lived at the edge of town. He was a loner who knew a lot about cars. He also had a creative mind with a bit of a twist. We were 11 or 12 years old at the time. Bill and I found the Eagle Racer, gassed it up and to my amazement he got it started. It had internal roll bars, no seats and, more importantly, no brakes. Bill's knowledge seemed deficient in that area. We used a five-gallon bucket for a seat and decided not to worry about the brakes—at least initially! We took off around town at low speed, coasting around turns and easing through stop signs (there were no stoplights in Bentonville at that time). Neither of us had a driver's license or, for that matter, knew much about driving!

"Oh my God, I can't stop!"

"Oh shit, slow down."

"Look out for that guy crossing the street!"

We were out of control!

We yelled and waved at cars and people to stop, to move, to look out. It was crazy. We were laughing and scared at the same time. We learned we could shift into reverse, albeit with a lot of gear grinding and let the clutch out to stop. Smoke and a burning smell belched from the clutch, but it slowed the car.

God takes care of little boys. Thanks, God! We made it back, parked the Eagle Racer to resume rusting in the rain and no one was hurt. WHEW! Great day!!

Like I said, Bill Black was clever, creative and a little twisted. One day he came by my house.

"Mike, I gotta show you something." Parked outside was his family's car, an olive green 1950 Ford, the one that was shaped like a turtle and had the color to match.

We took off down West Central. Bill turned off the ignition key, pumped the accelerator several times and turned the key back on. A huge BANG!!! erupted from the rear of the car. It made my heart stop. We soon realized this was fun. We cruised around town until we found some unsuspecting soul quietly walking along the sidewalk enjoying the beautiful summer weather and…key off, pump, pump, pump, key on…*BANG!!!*

Figure 19 - The Eagle Racer backfiring

People thought they were being shot. They dropped their grocery bags, threw their hands in the air, screamed "Lord Jesus!" Bill and I laughed until we cried.

As good as Ford mufflers were, they couldn't take this kind of abuse and the muffler finally split open. This decreased the "BANG" to only a dull thud.

The Midas Muffler Company had just arrived in Bentonville with their "guaranteed muffler replacement for the life of your car." Bill took them up on their offer and got a new one. We were back in business.

We rode around town at night and...*BANG!!!!* Flames shot three feet from the tailpipe. This terrified those unsuspecting citizens who were quietly walking home from the picture show. In addition to thinking they were shot, the flash of flames added another assault on the senses.

"What in the hell are you doing!? You can't do that!" We could hear them screaming for half a city block. We scared a dozen or more people before the muffler failed again. However, this time the friendly Midas man wasn't so friendly.

"I don't know what you boys are doing to these mufflers, but this is the last one I'm putting on for free, guarantee or no guarantee."

"Yes, sir." Shucks, we were having so much fun!

First Real Job

Excitement filled me when I started my first real job in 1959. I worked two summers for 35 cents an hour. The first summer I was only 15, too young to get a Social Security card, but the second summer I paid $7 withholding on my $263 summer pay. Not great pay, but the money didn't matter. Having mowed the neighbors' lawns for many years, this was my first real job.

Roy's Office Supply sold supplies in the front half of the store; in the rear were a repair area and printing shop. My job was cleaning typewriters and sweeping the floors. By the end of the school year all of the typewriters needed to be cleaned, lubricated and adjusted.

Roy Scroggins, the owner, worked up front, waiting on customers and writing up printing orders. "Mr. Wizard," my boss, repaired and adjusted every type of office machine. He was magic to me and took the time to explain how adding machines worked.

In the printing shop, "Mr. Printer" had three printing presses and a typecase holding metal type. He picked out individual letters and placed them in hand-held composing "sticks," which were then assembled in galleys for the presses. Single sheets of paper were placed one-by-one in the press and removed after the printer cycled.

On my first day, Mr. Wizard explained that my job was to remove the old ribbons, rubber platens and feet from the typewriters and carry the machines to the back room to be soaked in cleaning tanks.

"Mike, you must try to avoid Mr. Printer when he's working."

"Okay, Mr. Wizard." My excitement to get started overcame my curiosity about his request.

The largest of the three presses was positioned in front of the door to the back room. If Mr. Printer was on one side of the press, I could avoid him by walking on the other side. That was simple enough.

However, the plan didn't work as I had hoped. The typewriters weighed 25 pounds and were awkward to carry. Quite often, Mr. Printer moved into my chosen path, requiring me to back up and go around the other way. We never spoke, but his looks told me I was in his space and not welcome. I did my best to stay out of his way.

In the back room were three stainless steel tanks. Each was two feet square and two thirds full with Varsol, a nonflammable hydrocarbon solvent. When working alone I would talk to the typewriters: "Okay, little guy, time for your swim."

I would invert the typewriter for its "dive" into the first pool. After a few up-and-down backstrokes, I'd set it gently on the bottom of the pool. The liquid would remove the dirt and dried lubrication. While it soaked, I retrieved another machine from the front. I gave the submerged machine a few more shakes, drained it, dipped it into pool number two for a rinse and then submerged it into tank number three to be lubricated with oil. After allowing the typewriter to drain, I placed it on the floor atop heavy craft paper to dry overnight. The next day they were reunited with their rubber and plastic parts and awarded a new ribbon by Mr. Wizard.

I repeated this process daily until the school typing room was filled with refurbished machines ready for the hunt-and-peck techniques of new typing students. Near the end of the summer, with my work completed, Roy Scroggins asked that I follow him to the back room. We stood staring at the tanks.

"Mike, we have to change the Varsol in the tanks. Here's a five gallon bucket."

"Yes, Mr. Roy." I paused. "Where do 'we' dump it?"

At first he looked puzzled, then walked to the door that opened onto the alley and looked up and down.

"Dump it out there," he said, pointing to the asphalt alley with a wide wave of his hand. He didn't look like he was too sure about this, but I assumed "the boss" was right. I thought the Varsol would just trickle down the alley and disappear. I had seen heavy rains do the same thing many times.

After the first dump I noticed this was not at all like rainwater running down the alley. The asphalt was hot from the August sun. Most of the Varsol ran down the left wheel rut. The straw colored liquid became black as it flowed down the alley. I guessed it was just picking up a little color from the grease and oil.

It took over thirty dumps to empty the three tanks. I didn't pay much attention to the alley after the first few dumps and just focused on getting the job done. After I finished I looked more carefully. The 80 gallons of Varsol had only progressed down the alley about a hundred feet and left large black puddles along its path. The asphalt dissolved where the solvent first hit, leaving only gravel.

Oh my, I thought.

While standing in the doorway surveying the mess, a white pickup drove through the puddles, covering his tires and fenders in slime and stopped. A man stepped out of the truck, bent down, touched the black slurry and smelled it. Looking up, he saw a kid holding a bucket.

"What in the hell are you doing?"

"I'm getting rid of the old Varsol used to clean typewriters."

He started to speak, then shook his head and drove away.

Roy had been getting complaints on the phone. He called me to the back room and was shocked at the mess. Appearing agitated, he started to speak.

"I didn't mean…"

Then he stopped, realizing I had done what he had instructed me to do. He asked me to rake some dirt over the mess and that was the end of it. Roy was a fair man.

Every typewriter in Bentonville was clean, the tanks refilled and the alley mostly recovered. I needed something more to do.

Figure 20 - Getting rid of the old Varsol

The floor surrounding the printing presses was littered with paper. All summer long I had seen Mr. Printer toss whole sheets of paper directly onto the floor while he was printing, making no attempt to hit the trashcan. Why? It seemed rude. Taught not to question adults, I didn't ask.

"Mr. Wizard, could I sweep the floor?"

Looking up from his Remington calculator, he surveyed the accumulated paper, which extended into our repair shop and even the sales area.

"Yes, but Mike don't disturb…"

"Yes, I know. I won't bother Mr. Printer."

I surveyed the task. The paper was two inches thick in some places, covering the metal feet of the presses and type case that held the metal type for each job. The paper looked like snowdrifts around a tree or garden wall. I naïvely began with a push broom. This was ineffective at dislodging the layers of paper, although I managed to create a two-foot high mound against the back room door. Mr. Printer looked on without verbal comment, but his expression spoke more.

He had tolerated me walking through his space, but now I was disturbing his paper firma. I ushered the initial pile into the back room and deposited it in a large trash barrel. The remaining paper formed a colorful mosaic of every color, shape and size. Another method was needed to finish the job. I decided to pick up the papers with my hands, gathering up as much as I could hold and dumping the refuse into an empty box. Gradually I exposed the concrete floor, which was nearly black from years of being covered with inky paper.

As I continued to pick up paper, something shiny and jingly fell to the floor—several rings holding twenty or thirty keys. Before I could examine them further, Mr. Printer grabbed the keys from me without a word. They disappeared into his pocket and he returned to his press. He moved so fast he hadn't missed a cycle of his printing.

Mr. Wizard observed this event without turning his head, but remained silent.

I stood there stunned, wondering what had happened. *Wow,* I thought, *did I do something wrong?* It was the end of the day and everyone went home without saying a word.

On arrival, my mother asked, "Mike, are you okay? You look troubled."

"Mom, sometimes I don't understand adults."

"Did you do anything wrong?"

"No, I don't think so. Maybe tomorrow I'll figure it out."

I arrived at 8:30 the next morning and Mr. Wizard was already at his workbench. We were alone. He called me over.

"Mike, Mr. Printer had been looking everywhere for those keys for the last six months. It has caused him great worry and he really appreciates you finding them. But he may not be able to tell you so."

"Okay, Mr. Wizard." But I still didn't understand.

Mr. Printer arrived shortly thereafter and went to work. Later that morning I walked toward the back room. He suddenly stopped his press, looked at me and said, "Mike, thank you for finding my keys."

Had he spoken to me? Did he actually say, "Thank you"? Surprised, all I could say was, "Yes, sir."

However, that was not the end but rather the beginning. From then on he began asking me to help carry reams of paper to his station wagon for deliveries and to get things from the back room. One day as I was watching his printing press operate, he stopped, looked at me and explained its operation.

"Mike, when the press is running it continues unless I stop it. I must remove the printed sheet, inspect it for proper alignment or smudges and place a new sheet for the next cycle. If the sheet I remove is not perfect, I throw it on the floor. There's no time to hit the trashcan. Also, I must keep my hands clean so I don't smudge the next sheet. That's why there's so much paper on the floor. Mike, thank you for cleaning it up."

"You're welcome, Mr. Printer. Thank you for explaining."

Suddenly I felt bad for thinking he was rude. Now it made perfect sense—it was how he kept up with the speed of the press.

A week later he invited me to his home for dinner. His wife was a delightful person and as we finished dinner she spoke, "Bruce, please get the apple cobbler out of the oven and ice cream from the freezer."

"Of course, dear."

After dessert we sat in the living room and talked. I found out they were unable to have children.

As I was leaving, Mrs. Printer said, "Mike, it has been very hard for us not having children, especially for Bruce. He's from a large family, all boys."

A few days later, while helping him carry reams of paper to his station wagon, I told him canary yellow was my favorite color.

"Mike, yellow is my favorite color, too."

Manure and Mischief

Vol Lindsey was a successful attorney in Bentonville. At the time I didn't really know what attorneys were or what they did. That may seem like an amazing statement, but why should a nine-year-old kid in a tiny town in the Ozark Mountains in 1953 know anything about attorneys? My parents weren't divorced, we weren't bankrupt and no one in our family or anyone we knew had been in jail or even accused of anything (besides getting drunk occasionally, but Dad had considerable company in that endeavor and sometimes it was Vol himself at the Wednesday night poker games).

Mr. Lindsey lived six doors down from us on West Central Avenue. He had a large corner lot extending back to 2nd Street. He kept his trotting horse in a small corral and stable toward the back of the lot. In years past he raced a surrey at the local racetrack. One day he let me sit in the surrey, but my feet couldn't reach the footrests. I couldn't imagine being inches away from the pounding hooves of a horse running at top speed. It had to have been exciting. The surrey racing had ended, but Vol kept the trotter. She was like an old friend, something in life you don't sell.

We were young kids hanging out at the local hamburger and ice cream joint with nothing to do on a summer night and boredom prompted us to entertain ourselves. We didn't have television, so we turned to pranks for entertainment. And Vol's horse provided the props for our pranks.

The first was a classic Halloween prank. This involved filling a paper bag with rather fresh horse manure and placing it on someone's front porch. The "someone" was usually one of those people who turned on the porch light, came out and wanted to look at your costume when you came by trick or treating. Didn't they know it was supposed to be dark and scary? All we wanted was the candy. Therefore, they needed to be punished.

We would place the manure-filled bag on the front pouch and light the top of the bag with a match. All but one of us would retreat to the nearby bushes. When the top was burning well, the lookout would knock on the door and run to join the others. Invariably the homeowner would come out and start stomping the bag.

Oh my!

We were long gone by then, but could hear the uncontrolled ravings of the poor victim. In some cases, their rage might have been therapeutic.

I came up with the idea for our second manure prank. We revisited Vol's trotter's territory for another fresh load. I also obtained an old purse from my mother. I can't remember what I told her I needed it for. (For all her wisdom, she was rather trusting of our activities and gave us free reign for whatever life had to offer. The alternative approach is to think you can monitor and control your kids' activities, which, of course, you can't.)

We filled the purse with the "freshest ingredients available" (sounds like an ice cream commercial). We went downtown to Zesto's, the hamburger joint. We placed the loaded purse at the edge of the road between the First Baptist Church and Carl Burger's used car lot.

We retreated to Zesto's, where we stood innocently observing the outcome of placing the bait. How would people react? What was the true nature of Bentonville's citizens?

Well, the first car that passed by stopped. The passenger got out, grabbed the purse and the car sped away. Fifty feet down the road the purse sailed out the window, along with screams and cuss words. We laughed and laughed.

We repeated the prank several more times. I'm sure most people were just trying to return the purse to its rightful owner. Then one car drove back and parked directly in front of Zesto's. This big guy slowly got out of his car. By the expression on his face he wasn't going to order a hot fudge sundae.

"Which of you kids knows anything about a purse across the street?"

"What purse? We don't know anything about that, sir."

"That's good."

He got back in his car and slowly drove away.

"Well, it's getting late, better get home," I said.

All agreed it was enough for one night.

A Black Eye I Didn't Deserve

Like many small towns close together, there was a rivalry between Bentonville and Rogers. The two towns were only seven miles apart via Highway 71, with Rainbow Curve near the halfway point. They were called "sister cities," but "brother cities" would have been more appropriate considering the way we got along. The rivalry usually centered on sports, especially football, but it advanced to other things.

In the 1950s, Rogers had a slightly greater population at around 4,000 and was actually growing slowly. Rogers had the Daisy Air Rifle manufacturing plant and other new companies and was prospering, but this was relative to Arkansas standards of the time. Bentonville, even though it was the county seat, was slowly dying.

Towns have personalities. Rogers had an unfriendly, even aggressive temperament. Bentonville had a quiet, friendly, slow-paced ambience, which was probably why businesses were slowly dying. The kids took on the personalities of their towns. Kids from Rogers were rather mean and violent. I think some of them had real grown-up type jobs before or after school, such as catching chickens.

Catching chickens is the process of pulling grown chickens from their warm and roomy chicken houses, cramming them into small wooden cages and trucking them off to the processing plant. Everyone knows chickens aren't very smart, but they didn't need smarts to know who the enemy was. The guys picked up the chickens by one leg and carried 10-15 of them upside down between the fingers of one hand. Needless to say, the birds would furiously resist their captors with every beak and claw at their disposal. What the chickens lacked in size they made up for in numbers. The Society for the Prevention of Cruelty to Animals was not around to referee.

Then the catchers would open the cage door and coax them into death row. There was pride among them about how many chickens they could carry at one time. It is clear we Americans will compete for or about anything, although I'm not aware of any national competition in this event.

Hundreds of flapping, pecking, clawing and pooping chickens made this job my greatest fear. It motivated me to do my homework and aspire to a job requiring brains and not a vise grip. At the time, catching chickens paid very well and openings were always available.

I don't know if all the mean boys from Rogers were chicken catchers, but they set the tone for the rest. On Halloween they would get crates of rotten eggs and tomatoes and cruise around Bentonville, lobbing missiles at our cars and innocent bystanders. I got a tomato in the back of my head standing at the local hangout ordering a cherry coke (better than a rotten egg, to be sure). I like to think our Bentonville mischief was more sophisticated than their mindless hostility; besides, we didn't have access to any rotten produce.

Generally we didn't date girls from Rogers, but I dated two. One was Dietra, a very tall and attractive girl with a moderately large-sized frame. She was 16 going on 22 and much more mature than I was at the time. I think she wanted me to "try something," but I was unnerved by how big she was and how assertive she acted.

The other Rogers girl I dated was Sue, a short, cute, bubbly, talkative girl who was usually fun to be with. One night Bill Black and I were out on a double date. We all had a couple of beers but Sue had a lot more to drink and shortly thereafter commenced to vomit. This was a clear sign the fun was over and time to take Sue home. We waited in her driveway until the latest heave subsided and I helped her the rest of the way to her house. I thought she was done being sick, but upon arrival at the front door she threw up into a potted azalea on the front porch. This roused her mother, who expressed her displeasure with this turn of events in no uncertain terms. I made a feeble apology and retreated to the refuge of Bill Black's 1950 Ford.

Unfortunately for me, Sue's brother was a friend of one of the chicken catchers. They usually worked at night, but alas it was Saturday. Two of Roger's finest chicken catchers caught up with us just past Rainbow Curve on Highway 71 and forced us off the road. They accused me of getting Sue drunk and taking advantage of her. I was starting to deny this accusation when a left hook struck my right cheek and knocked me onto the trunk of Bill's car. I rallied to attempt a few swings, but it was a hopeless attempt. Chicken catchers may not

be bright, but they are strong and mean.   I had been a complete
gentleman with Sue, but sustained a chipped tooth and a black eye.

My only solace is that they're most likely still catching chickens.
I, on the other hand, have moved on to non-poultry related work.
(Although I still have the chipped tooth.)

Bentonville Ice Hockey

Every winter a "Blue Northern" came down from Canada and temperatures stayed in the teens for several days. People's pipes froze, but more important to us the pond froze and we played ice hockey—Arkansas style.

The "duck pond," as it was known, was southwest of town, about a third the size of a football field. We boys would bike out there and play ice hockey, using sticks from the nearby woods, a smashed up can for a puck and our shoes for ice skates. The goals were a pair of rocks at each end of the pond. We would slide around on the ice, whacking the puck and each other, until the sun went down and we rode our bikes home.

The pond was located in what is now the south parking lot of the corporate headquarters of Wal-Mart. The pond was 150 feet due south from the main entrance. Times change.

Figure 21 - Hockey on the pond

Cucumbers, Orange Vodka and Alka-Seltzer

Cucumbers, orange vodka and Alka-Seltzer were the near demise of Jimmy, David and me, respectively. As some boys do in high school, we did a little experimenting with drinking in the 1960's.

William Blake said long ago, "One must know what is too much before he can know how much is enough." Although we didn't know who Blake was, that was our approach to experimentation.

Jimmy and I went out one night and we drank several cans of Schlitz Malt Liquor. We were parked in the rear of Zesto's parking lot, the local hangout, where it was dark, but we could see the cars as they drove through. We were collecting data on who was dating whom.

Jimmy continued to partake at a record pace and ended up vomiting. It was clear the fun was over for the evening. It was time to take Jimmy home!

I was in a little better shape and able to drive (yeah, right). Anyway, we made it to Jimmy's house and I was walking him to his bed via the side door when Big Jim (Jimmy's dad) appeared. Oh shit! Little Jim staggered to the bathroom to drive the porcelain bus and call Earl, Ralph and Uncle for the umpteenth time…and I was left with Big Jim. This was a very uncomfortable encounter, given the circumstances. An eternity passed before he calmly remarked, "It must have been those cucumbers Jimmy had with dinner that made him sick."

"Yes sir," I quickly agreed, "I think that's it. I better go help him."

Since Benton County was (and still is) dry, one night David and I got someone to buy us some orange vodka. One might surmise our level of sophistication from our choice of beverage and the fact that we would then mix it with Coca-Cola.

David and I were driving around, checking who was out and about, while drinking the potent mix. It didn't seem to sit too well with him.

"Pull over," he urgently requested.

I immediately pulled into the parking lot of the First Christian Church on Second Street. David had eaten a hamburger steak and French fries at Zelda's café and he left quite a mess for the faithful churchgoers, for the next day was Sunday.

David felt better and wanted to go see his true love, Meza. He rinsed his mouth out with some straight Coca-Cola and washed his face in the water fountain at Zesto's. We drove to Meza's house and parked in the driveway. David got out of the car and staggered to the door, knocked and was suddenly hit by another wave of nausea. He was heaving off the edge of the porch when Walter Grimes (Meza's dad) came to the door and turned on the light. Mr. Grimes quickly assessed the situation and suggested David go home.

"Yes, sir, I must have the stomach flu."

Then it was my turn. I can't remember what I drank, but it was enough to get me sick and wanting to go home. When we got there, it took some help from David to ascend the spiral staircase. At least I wasn't vomiting.

I knew I was going to feel bad the next day, so David put two Alka-Seltzer tablets in a glass of water. I grabbed the glass and chugged them down. Problem was, the tablets weren't dissolved. Whereupon I began to belch...big time.

I never could swallow air and belch-talk like some people could; at least, not until that night. I could have recited the Ten Commandments, the Boy Scout Motto and the Declaration of Independence and never have taken a breath!

Chapter Five

More Colorful People

Lightnin' Jim

According to the townsfolk, Lightnin' Jim got his name from being too close to a lightning strike. He had straight, paper white hair that stuck out in all directions. There were no physical marks on him from a lightning strike, at least that I could see, but there must have been some internal damage because Jim was definitely different.

Lightnin' Jim was convinced we were running out of wood (or soon would, no pun intended). One never knows where people get these ideas, but he was convinced, or some said possessed, that in just a few years all the trees would be gone and he had to hoard a supply of this very valuable commodity.

Jim lived at the edge of town with no close neighbors. This relative isolation allowed him to create his own world. He had a small two-story house on a large lot. The two stories served him well.

Jim drove an old green pickup truck that produced billows of gray smoke. He drove at 10 m.p.h. all around town, his head frantically jerking from side to side, scouting for wood nobody wanted. Any kind of wood—branches, old boards, wooden crates and boxes were all treasures that would soon make him rich. The rear of his pickup was piled high with the findings of the day. People passed the word to him when they had some scrap wood and he hauled it to his house (or "hoard," as some said).

His lot, which extended back a full block to the next street, was entered from the right side of his house. Stacks of gray weathered pallets on the right and a mountain of empty fruit crates on the left formed the entrance. Here began a literal maze of wood extending up eight feet or more, with numerous forks, turns and intersections covering his entire property. The wood was neatly stacked and sorted by type, length, width and thickness. Branches were neatly bound into bundles and laid in rows of four across and ten or more high. The stacks towered well above the first floor windows of his house.

Jim's maze didn't allow a view of more than the next turn or intersection. Once inside, you had little sense of where you had been or where you were going or how to get through it or how to get out.

I remember the first time I entered his maze. It was like walking into a forest. I made a few turns and crossed a few intersections, utterly fascinated by what I saw. Then I realized I was lost. I backtracked the way I thought I came in, only to hit a dead end. I remember being a little frightened that I was trapped.

Figure 22 - Lost in the maze

I didn't panic, but backtracked more and found my friend David, who looked a little concerned as well. We worked together to figure a way out. One of us stood at an intersection while the other explored in one direction or another, eventually finding the exit. Once we got out, we confessed our mutual fears of the experience.

"David, that was a little scary. I thought for a little while that we wouldn't get out."

"Me too, Mike. Do you want to go back in?"

"No, it's getting late, we wouldn't want to get caught in there at night."

David agreed. "We'll come back another day."

We did go back a few times.

Jim's maze was different from a real maze. A real one is designed to be complex, but allows for a final passage through persistence and trial and error. Jim's maze had no clear passage through. In addition, Jim's maze evolved randomly from his continuing need to find more space. When he ran out of vacant land, he built up. When he ran out of space, the higher and the less organized the stacks became. He had no equipment other than a few ladders, a wheelbarrow and a pull cart to transport the treasures.

Indeed, the higher the stack became, the more difficult it was to go even higher and the less precise placement could be. But overall, the stacks were tidy, even when eight feet high.

Jim's maze was designed, if you will, by his random walking. He pushed a wheelbarrow or cart of wood, all the while looking for a space above to hold his new treasure. In his mind he was creating walls of wealth that would soon make him a rich man. It was just a matter of time.

One day David and I entered his maze. Lightnin' Jim came running out.

"What are you boys doing over there by those strawberry flats?" he cried. "I just got them last week."

He was obviously concerned we were going to steal them and undercut his prices, when one day he would have a world monopoly on his product. It was only a matter of time.

Jim died a few years later. He had no wife and children to inherit his fortune. The city of Bentonville became responsible for his house and maze of accumulated treasure. Initially, they built a fence across the front of his property to keep people out, but when his estate settled everything was trucked to the Bentonville landfill. That's where it lies buried today. I'm sure Jim regretted not living long enough to reap the fortune he had created. His time ran out before the trees did.

Smoky Dacus

Any discussion of colorful Bentonville people must include Smoky Dacus. In 1954, Smoky curtailed his musical career to host the morning show broadcast on KAMO 1390 AM. This was the first local radio station in Bentonville and Rogers. He played country music and broadcast the news, weather, farm commodity prices and upcoming events. He loudly slurped his coffee on the air for all to hear, accompanied by an even louder "ah" or "good coffee."

Smoky was very popular and today would be a "radio personality." I remember nothing of his humor or politics; however, in those days everyone was a Democrat since people still remembered the Depression and FDR. People wanted to forget those hard times and eventually did and now the state is staunchly Republican.

Marvin Strange: Daredevil to the End

Marvin Strange wasn't strange, just a daredevil. He was a master of fixing motorcycles and cars, which was a good thing, because he was always crashing them. His body always had abrasions or a cast on one extremity or another. He lived on the edge of town near the old Park Springs Hotel and his yard was full of motorcycles and cars in various states of disassembly.

Marvin was always happy, smiling and laughing. He was enjoying his life. We went water skiing at Lake Bella Vista and he managed to run into the side of the island. His skis stuck into the steep bank and Marvin flew onto the flat grassy area above. We turned the boat around in time to see him smiling and unhurt. He really seemed to have enjoyed it. He clearly pushed life's throttle to the limit, with little or no fear of anything. It was to be his downfall.

After high school I lost track of Marvin but heard he moved to Missouri and had a successful construction company. He took up flying. He and his family were killed flying in bad weather from Missouri to Bentonville in his private plane.

I could have told them not to give Marvin a pilot's license, but I have no doubt he was smiling and fully expected to survive the crash.

The Sisk Brothers

The human body is supposed to be upright, eyes straight, looking at you, shoulders, head and neck square and symmetrical, the back straight. Good posture that is normal and natural.

The bodily appearance of the Sisk Brothers was somewhat difficult to behold. Their backs and necks were fixed such that they were looking at their own feet. They could not straighten their necks or backs. A person facing them would only see the tops of their heads. You couldn't see their eyes. In order to look forward, they adjusted their bodies' position in several ways and did other maneuvers to compensate.

First, they would stand sideways. Second, since they couldn't rotate their heads, they stood tiptoe on one foot to elevate that side of their bodies. Even this permitted them to see only a little further in front of them. With their eyes looking to that side (that is, looking "forward"), their upper eyelids blocked their view. To see further, they would raise their upper eyelids with their index fingers so it wouldn't block their view.

These contortions were appalling to watch, especially since they were trying to accomplish something so simple that we take for granted every day.

Their disease was a progressive one. Unknown at the time, they had ankylosing spondylitis, a severe form of arthritis. They were relatively normal when, at 17, they joined the U.S. Army during the Korean War and likely struggled through boot camp. But during this time their spine inflammation and pain rapidly progressed. After a few months of service they were deemed unfit for duty and given honorable medical discharges. They had served our country to the fullest extent they could.

Given their physical limitations, one would think that they wouldn't be able to do any useful work or employment. Not true. In a seated position and leaning back, they could look forward with both eyes, no contortions needed. So what gainful occupation did they pursue?

Enter the Sisk Brother's Taxi Company. Two older cars sat in their driveway at the corner of North Main St. and C Street N.E. "Sisk Brother's Taxi" was written on the doors of their cars. They were the only taxi service in Bentonville and transported those unable to drive themselves. In the process, they helped others with disabilities different from their own.

Mule Meat Brown and Shorty Parish

When I was a kid there were two people who drove horse or mule-drawn wagons in Bentonville. Mule Meat Brown drove the "good wagon" and Shorty Parish the "bad wagon." Despite his nickname, Mule Meat Brown had a horse drawn, well-kept wagon. He lived southwest of town and my friend David Johnson said he would see him coming by his house and turn down C Street to the feed store. I don't know much about Mule Meat or how he got his name. With regard to his mode of transportation, I think he just preferred a wagon to a truck to haul feed and other supplies.

Shorty Parish had the "bad wagon" and he marched, or rather rolled to the tune of a different drummer. His wagon was an old open flat wagon, drawn by a mule, with no two wheels of the same size or type. They were rubber car tires rather than wagon wheels. The bed of the wagon was tilted front to back and from right to left. When Shorty was sitting in the seat he had to lean to the left and arch his back to be upright, but it didn't seem to bother him.

My best memory of Shorty was in the hot summers when he hauled block ice in my neighborhood for people who still had iceboxes. He would come up the alley between the Davis's and Mrs. Jackson's and stop. Shorty was, well...disheveled at best. Old straw hat, dirty, threadbare clothes and worn-out shoes.

Figure 23 – Shorty's mule

I wasn't sure who passed the straw hats down to whom, since Shorty's and the mule's hats were both stained brown with sweat and dirt. But then I realized the mule's ears protruded through holes at the junction of the brim and crown, so Shorty got them first since his hat had no holes. The mule was docile enough and stopped in the same place without any visible pull of the reins or verbal instructions from Shorty.

Numerous flies circled around the mule's rump and nose, but they seemed content to remain in those areas and not check our sweat or odor. The mule's coat was coarse and didn't beckon us to pet him (or her, I never knew which and wasn't compelled to ask).

Shorty would get out of the wagon and chuckle and frown at the three or four of us surrounding the back of his wagon. He didn't say much, but would chip small hand-sized pieces of ice for each of us. How wonderful it was in the hot summer! We would suck on the ice and rub it on our faces and bodies. He would carry blocks into my family's home, Mrs. Jackson's house, then the Davis's and we would wait for a possible second serving, usually denied as he muttered there would be nothing left if he gave it all to us. Yes, a simple summer delight—I can feel the cold on my forehead and ice water running down my cheeks like it was yesterday.

Shorty's other job was hauling garbage and "slop" to his hogs. Everyone knows that the worst thing that can happen to you is to have a hog farmer move in next door or upwind because hogs smell so bad.

Figure 24 - Shorty delivering ice

Most smells you get accustomed to and don't smell anymore, but hog manure always smells bad.

On the wagon bed just behind Shorty's seat was several empty wooden buckets of every size and description, but they shared one thing—all had dried goo on their sides. During the school year Shorty would pick up discarded food from our school cafeteria every afternoon.

One day I was there when he made his pick up. Shorty carefully poured the slop from a large can into his buckets like it was fine French wine.

"Mr. Parish," I said, "that slop is the most disgusting stuff I've ever seen."

He just looked at me with even greater disgust and said, "The hogs love it."

Then he muttered something I couldn't understand, but it didn't sound complimentary.

Chapter Six

Closing Stories

My Sojourn Back to Arkansas

Having been born in 1944 in the Ozark Mountains makes me an Arkansas hillbilly, pure and simple. Furthermore, my speech labels me as being from the southern states. Arkansas has been viewed as a state full of slow, backward, ignorant, behind-the-times people for most of the 20th century. My old friend, Kester Evans, born in 1900, brought this up once when we were talking.

Kester knew why Arkansas was singled out. The widely read book *Slow Train Through Arkansas*, published in 1903, established the connection between backwardness and my state. Seven million copies sold at twenty-five cents each. In his book *Hillbilly*, author Anthony Harkins also cites *Slow Train* as the origin of Arkansas myths. He adds that the book had "very little to do with Arkansas or southern mountains and is largely a haphazard retelling of standard jokes, puns and minstrel stage quips." None of that mattered and the connection was made.

Hillbilly focused on the origin of the word and the location of hillbillies, which includes Appalachia, the mountainous regions of intervening states and the Ozark Mountains. Radio and television programs, including *Ma and Pa Kettle* and *The Beverly Hillbillies* perpetuated the stereotypes and they stuck on the Ozarks and me.

I remember teachers discussing a third grade reader with illustrations of where hillbillies lived. The teachers recognized that Bentonville fell in the defined area. Of more concern to them was the derogatory depiction of hillbillies as ignorant, backward and unsophisticated.

Few people grow up without some stereotype based on their racial, ethnic, or regional origins and I could have done far worse than my Arkansas hillbilly label.

After high school, college and medical school in Arkansas and then an internship in Texas, I joined the U.S. Navy and was stationed in Connecticut, Washington, D.C., Florida, the San Francisco Bay Area and then North Lake Tahoe. I practiced ER medicine for 37 years.

When my ER patients got to know me, they'd ask where I was from. I saw their question as a compliment—they liked me and were comfortable asking me a personal question. I told them where I was from and if I felt like entertaining myself, I may have added, "I'm an Arkansas hillbilly." This usually stunned them and required them to digest the information carefully.

"Okay, he's a physician...check."

"He knows his stuff...check."

"I like the way he's taking care of me (or my family)...check."

"Now, he said he's an Arkansas hillbilly... check."

"Well, this Arkansas hillbilly I like."

We both chuckled a bit and I smiled and nodded my head. Shortly thereafter, they would laugh and realize I had set them up. It was fun.

But there have been other times when people judged me by the way I talked. Generally, I saw that as their problem and wasn't disturbed by their quick judgment. They just didn't know me yet. There are few of us "talk funnies" left, as kids today learn speech patterns from watching television and not from their parents, who are now both working.

My old friend Kester lived 97 years into the 20th century, so he saw and heard all the hillbilly stereotypes. According to him, it was Sam Walton's success that did the most to change these views.

In my opinion, the negative stereotypes of rural, isolated areas were largely true during my youth. However, there were equally important advantages to growing up in rural, small-town America.

After the surprise, pain and conflict of the failure of my second marriage, I had lost control of my personal and professional lives. After my divorce in 2008, I needed to make a major change. I was alone and the fond memories of Arkansas and the friends I still knew were all I had. I left Tahoe and returned to northwest Arkansas with excitement and enthusiasm, determined that I could reconnect with old friends and make new ones. I believed an older and experienced ER physician could contribute something to the local hospital and ER. I felt my professional dream was coming into focus as well.

However, the move proved to be a huge mistake in several ways. Many things were changing in my life and many things had changed in ER medicine and medicine in general during my 37 years in northern California that I didn't appreciate until my return to my home state.

The hospital administrators in California let physicians practice medicine to best serve our patients. Two hospitals where I worked in northwest Arkansas were remarkably different in their approach.

I was fired from the first hospital because I didn't share the strong born-again religious views of the ER nurses. Yes, fired. Four days after I mentioned my lack of religious beliefs to a nurse, the ER Director called me at night and said she couldn't get the ER nurses to work with me and I was not to return to work. Until then I was enjoying everyone and they were enjoying me.

Religion in California is largely a non-issue, especially in the workplace. My firing took me by complete surprise. I moved on to a large hospital in the area, having learned to never mention religion or my spiritual beliefs.

I have always been a patient advocate and practiced medicine to best serve my patients. In California I did that and I was appreciated for those efforts. However, medicine elsewhere had changed. All ERs see a large number of uninsured and underinsured patients and this was more so in Arkansas than California. Also, navigating the maze of medical care is confusing and I have always tried to schedule needed follow-up care and imaging studies for patients when I could. However, after doing this for a few Arkansas patients, I received indirect notice from the hospital administrator that ER physicians were not to schedule appointments or imaging studies after patients were discharged from the ER.

Eventually, I was told to leave voluntarily from the second hospital or I would have been fired. This was the administrator's way of denying care to the uninsured. Another ER physician had been fired after tangling with the same hospital administrator. A few months after I left the ER Director left as well. Three caring physicians had left. A few months later, the hospital Board fired the administrator. Did the hospital board finally realize their responsibility was to care for *all* the people of their city? I left Arkansas after ten months, lived in Oregon for year and I now live in Scottsdale, Arizona.

Given my age and idealistic devotion to patient care, I was no longer suited to practice ER medicine. I have retired and spent my time finishing this book.

In summary, Thomas Wolfe was right: "You can't go home again." I like to think my sojourn back to Arkansas helped a hospital live up to the words written on their ER wall: "We treat patients the way we treat our family."

Arkansas will always be my home and what I experienced during my youth has served me well through my entire life. I'm an Arkansas hillbilly, pure and simple.

My Walnut Tree

Whenever I'm in Bentonville I go by to see "my" tree. It roughly marks my beginning on earth and I am responsible for it being on earth. Furthermore, it will be on this earth long after I'm gone.

It's natural to want to leave something to be remembered by or for. I have children to mark my having passed this way, but there is something about a static living thing that doesn't move around and whose only function, other than maintaining its own being, is to mark my prior existence. It's a little strange, but I like it and here is how it came to be.

My first work or chore as a child was mowing the family yard. I was probably eight or nine years old and it was the early 1950s. Our home was on a half-acre lot and every inch was covered with grass. Furthermore, grass grew well in the Arkansas summer, given the rain and warm climate and required cutting every one or two weeks.

Our lawnmower was a huge red Yazoo that easily outweighed me. The push handles were at my eye level. The Yazoo had large spoke-type rear wheels and small rubber front wheels. The blade was out front, connected to the engine by a belt. It was always hard to start and harder to push, especially for a scrawny kid.

Figure 25 - Preserving the walnut sapling

The truth was, I enjoyed mowing the lawn. When I finished, the yard looked good and gave me a sense of accomplishment and purpose. My brother and I were supposed to alternate on this chore, but he didn't enjoy it like I did, so I did it more often.

One hot day I was nearly finished mowing the backyard. I was at the rear of our property, next to the shrubs shielding our yard from 2nd Street. Among the blades of grass was a little sprout with a lighter green color than the surrounding grass. It seemed to be announcing to the world, "Hey, I'm new here! I haven't been around long enough to get really green yet."

It was no taller than the uncut grass. I made a little jog around the sprout and finished mowing.

A week later I mowed again and it was three inches high and I missed it again. It was greener and barely stood out among the blades of grass. My brother mowed the following week and cut its top off. By the next mowing, it was back to four inches and I jogged around it again. I showed it to my brother and he agreed to let it grow. By the end of the summer it was eight inches high and was clearly a little tree.

The following summer it continued to grow. During dry spells it started to turn brown, so I watered it every few days until it rained. I surrounded it with rocks to protect it. Over the next few years it grew and grew and Dad said it was a walnut tree. Dad thought one of the walnuts from Mrs. Tinnin's walnut tree had been plowed under when we had a garden in that spot. It had sprouted and there it was trying to make its way in the world, just like me.

Now, sixty years later, the tree is eighty feet high and its trunk is fifteen inches across. So far, we're both healthy.

Death Will Become Okay

I had an important conversation with my mother when she was 80 years old. She was blind from macular degeneration, had severe degenerative arthritis and underwent hip replacement surgery. She had outlived two husbands and her sister (her only sibling), lived alone in northwest Arkansas, but was financially secure. She could no longer drive, play bridge, or read books, her true passion. She adamantly refused to live near or with my brother or me. She "didn't want to be a burden." Her caring for her mother for fifty years, both financially and physically may have influenced this attitude. However, she never complained about this or anything else, being a woman of few words.

I was home visiting her and we were enjoying an evening cocktail. At that time I was approaching 50.

"Mom, this death thing is sort of scary to me. No one knows where we go. Life just ends."

Mother seemed ready for this discussion and came right back.

"Oh yes, Mike. It should scare you at your age—you're healthy, active, busy and enjoy your work and family." She paused.

"But Mike, at some point when you get older, death will become okay."

These were the few words I needed. I put aside my fears of death, knowing death would someday become okay. Why worry now? I could worry later, if I had to. But I don't think I'll need to.

Mother lived another nine years and I visited her frequently in the nursing home. I clearly remember my last visit before she died. At that time, I thought her mind was completely gone. I stood beside her bed, stroking her hair. She opened her blind eyes and looked toward me.

"Mike, I'm okay."

Those were the last words she ever spoke. She died a few weeks later. She had told me years before she was looking forward to seeing her father and sister when she passed.

When my end nears, I will look forward to seeing Mom again.

Fireflies

Letter for My Children

I'm sitting in the oldest part of the Bentonville Cemetery, between the graves of the first-generation Irish Haneys on my right and my parents to my distant left. I like this cemetery. It's quiet and sunny to the very end of the day. Secluded, yes, but I could throw a rock and hit the home offices of Wal-Mart Stores.

Seven-thirty in the evening, one day short of the longest day in 2009. I have brought a chair, my journal, some whiskey and a cigar. Songbirds sing, there's a gentle breeze, it's very peaceful and I love being here with my family. I have my parents and all my ancestors with me. However, I really mean *within me*, which is where they are. Strange? Well, perhaps.

Their spirits are not in these graves. Their souls, their being, their continued existence is in me. They see through my eyes and express themselves through me. There is no other place they exist.

In their living, my ancestors carried those who went before. Then each and all passed on to the next generation and I have them now. The life I have is so much better and fuller because they worked hard, sacrificed so much, learned so much. I am the fruit of their toil. I know some of their individual gifts and I have written what I know. I thank them all.

Figure 26 - Fireflies glowing in the graveyard

My children know my beliefs. This is not new to them. They will have our ancestors and me, at the end of my time. Remember us all. Being remembered is our immortality!

I light my cigar and freshen my drink. The sun has set. I look up from my journal toward the graves of my parents to see an amazing sight. Tens of thousands of fireflies! Looking in all directions, I see fireflies as I've never seen them before. I am stunned.

They form a distinct layer of light, two feet thick, hovering about a foot off the ground. The band of light has a uniform thickness, following the rolling contour of the ground and extending in every direction. It is made up of tens of thousands of fireflies. They glow at the bottom of the layer, ascend lit for two seconds and then go dark at the top, descending unlit and unseen before beginning another luminescent ascent. I watch in disbelief as the band of light undulates against the dark grass and headstones and distant trees.

I ask myself, "Is this real? One drink at Jimmy Tinnin's home before I came and one here. I'm okay."

I look around. Yes, everything is as it was. How many are in this layer? Tens of thousands...a hundred thousand...yes! In front, behind, surrounding me are a hundred thousand fireflies. I am stunned, in wonderment. I have seen a lot of nature, but never nature in this spiritual form. Sixty-four years old and I have never seen such a sight.

Finally, I sit and just look. My mind races for understanding, meaning. Are these the spirits of the dead rising?

"Michael, wait. You know you already have their spirits."

My ancestors are seeing this as I am, through my eyes now...and what a show we see. I sit wide-eyed and unblinking.

Now the scientist in me steps forward. "Calculate the number of fireflies in one cubic foot. Michael, step back from the awe. Focus. Okay, 100-200 per cubic foot!"

Enough calculating, back to the show. I sit and look in wonder. I am baffled...does this happen every night? Okay, later I googled "fireflies."

Yes, this is a mating thing. Of course, why else would they cavort so? And, of course, it is only the males who are flying and flashing. Females are on the ground, bushes and trees, checking out the flashing males. So, a female sees something special in one of the male's luminescent displays and she flashes him, requesting a closer look. He flies closer, both shorten their frequency of flashes, closer, together now...yes...they mate...for hours! Morning comes, the ground is soft from recent rains and she lays their young to wait the beginning of new life. The eggs hatch in a few weeks and subsist in their larval glowworm form for many months, then metamorphose to create fireflies next summer.

Okay, okay, yes, this is no less than an orgy. In addition, he now has her preferred code. "Tomorrow night?" he asks. No response. He persists: "I'll be flashing."

She responds, "I'll see."

I think back to when I was a kid and caught all those flashing males flying around in my yard and kept them in a jar all night in my room. Yes, I had holes in the lid, with sticks and grass inside. Yes, I let them go in the morning...but just think how they felt all night. And then they had to wait until near dark the next day so the females could see their stuff. I didn't know.

Nine-fifteen. It's darker now. I can barely see to write. More fireflies drift higher out of the layer. My cigar is bitter now and the whiskey nearly gone. I can't see to write, but I will sit until dark. I could fall asleep, but I must look, so all can see through my open eyes.

Nine-thirty, far fewer now. Nearly everyone has found a mate tonight!

Dark. I continue to look, so all can see. I beg you will do the same for me, when I live on in you.

Acknowledgments

All my friends and family, for their encouragement. Special thanks to Linda Robinson, Carole Westby Harter, Al Desetta, my editor and for their encouragement, ideas, guidance and patience. Special thanks to Bonnie Belza for her expert organization, knowledge and assistance in the completion and submission of this book.

Sources

Much of the historical material in Chapter One concerning Bentonville comes from Goodspeed's *History of Benton, Washington, Carroll, Madison, Crawford, Franklin and Sebastian Counties, Arkansas . . . 1889.* Chicago, Illinois: Goodspeed Publishing Company.

The book *Images of America – Bentonville* by Monte Harris (2010, Charleston, South Carolina: Arcadia Publishing), provided memories of early Bentonville.

About the Author

After graduating from Bentonville High School in the class of 1962 with 73 students, Michael Knott attended college and medical school and then joined the U.S. Navy. After leaving the service, he practiced Emergency Medicine for 37 years, mainly in Truckee, California. Michael has four children and seven grandchildren. An avid runner, biker, rower and skier, he's now retired and lives in Scottsdale, Arizona. This is his first book. He can be reached at http://www.michaelmknott.com.

About the Illustrator

William David Martin is an artist, designer and illustrator whose designs and illustrations have been featured on album and magazine covers, tour books, posters, first day cover prints and in local galleries. He resides in New Jersey with his wife, two children and their West Highland Terrier Lilly. He can be contacted on his website at http://www.wdmdesigns.com.